# GO! FIGHT! WIN!

# GO! FIGHT! WIN!

The National Cheerleaders Association
Guide for Cheerleaders

## Betty Lou Phillips

PHOTOGRAPHS BY FRANCIS SHEPHERD

DELACORTE PRESS/NEW YORK

This guide is for you! Whether you're thinking about becoming a cheerleader, or among the one million teens who are already into the sport. We want to bring out the best in you!

Published by
Delacorte Press
1 Dag Hammarskjold Plaza
New York, N.Y. 10017

Manufactured in the United States of America
First printing

Library of Congress Cataloging in Publication Data

Phillips, Betty Lou.
  Go! Fight! Win!

  Includes index.
  SUMMARY: A guide for cheerleaders with tips on how to get selected, instructions for developing basic skills, and ideas for cheers, routines, stunts, and skits. Also includes information on conduct at games, body care, and first aid.
  1.  Cheerleading.
[1.  Cheerleading]  I.  Shepherd, Francis.
II.  National Cheerleaders Association.  III.  Title.
GV718.P46        371.8'9         79-53607
ISBN 0-440-02956-2
ISBN 0-440-02957-0 lib. bdg.

# Acknowledgments

I would like to thank the staff of the National Cheerleaders Association, especially Lawrence Herkimer, Gene Cason, Van Power, Lance Wagers, and Carol Pojezny.

I am also indebted to the nice people at Bonne Bell who acted as consultants on this book.

And there's more:

Donna Mendias, Patti Stephens, and Rachel Kaplan.

John Cooper, Barry Moss, Arthur Goddard, Dan Hart, Bill Hardin, Richard Whisenand, Charles Sanders, Mike Ereli, Dan Seely, Susie Peake, Kathy McAnelly, Hilary Frame, Sheri Coskey, Allison Ebert, Kelly Sutton, Hugh Robertson, Cliff Roberts.

Other people who deserve special thanks are James Kotora, Sandra and D. R. Keener, and Jim Quinn.

And last, but by no means least, Alice Bregman, Barbara Storey, Jim Bruce, Judy Gitenstein, and Cynthia Toher.

# Contents

# Introduction

So, you want to be a cheerleader. Great! Being a cheerleader can bring joy, notoriety, physical development, social development, and many other positive things. The opportunities that present themselves to a cheerleader during the season are almost unlimited, and they are unique. A person who develops the capacity to speak to an audience with authority, direct a crowd, feel its pulse, know how to sway it, and get a planned reaction from it has developed a valuable asset. The leadership qualities and all the numerous activities on and off the field that are required of a good cheerleader often can make a difference later in life; you've learned to be the president of the organization, rather than simply one of the members.

There are only a few students in each school who have the opportunity to serve as a cheerleader, so the status is very high. The requirements and the responsibilities that have to be assumed are equally high. Everything in life that is worthwhile and brings an honor has to be paid for with time and effort. Learning to plan activities, set goals, and then carry them out to their completion are skills that are valuable for us in life after school. You have an opportunity to learn these skills through the activities demanded of a good cheerleader.

Many ideas in this book will, if followed, help you to be elected a cheerleader as well as to do a very good job as a cheerleader. Different situations and regulations exist among the various parts of the country, so some of the suggestions cannot be used in total. Yet this book's theory and philosophy could be adapted to any individual school situation and still stay within the guidelines of specifics imposed by the various school systems.

The material contained in this book will not only be valuable to individual cheerleaders but also to faculty advisors and sponsors. Following the guidelines presented herein will help to keep the squad organized and functioning efficiently all during the season. There are enough new routines, stunts, skits, etc., in this book to keep your squad supplied with fresh presentations week after week so your student body will be amply impressed with "their" cheerleaders.

Adapt this volume of information to your mascot, your school name, your school colors, etc., and the football and basketball games at your school will take on an added dimension. You can cheer for other sports such as hockey, wrestling, and soccer. There are enough ideas in this book to adapt to almost any spectator sport.

Enthusiasm is one of the keys and is a contagious thing that transmits to others. I hope that you will read this book with enthusiasm and that it will kindle additional enthusiasm within you.

Lawrence R. Herkimer, President
National Cheerleaders Association, Inc.

# Trying Out and Getting Elected

*Who started all this yelling?* If you don't know, you're not alone. There is no record of exactly when or where cheerleading—or spiritleading, as it is also known today—originated. It's believed to date back to ancient times, when crowds of people lined the roads, cheering to welcome home their warriors. One fact, however, is clear. Cheering never attracted interest until the early 1860s, when it began at competitive events on Ivy League campuses. Then it spread quickly through America. But this now grand old tradition wasn't organized until near the turn of the century, when the first "yell marshall," John Campbell, was elected at the University of Minnesota.

Of course, cheerleading was very different then. In those days, all a cheerleader had to do was direct a crowd in a simple recitation, such as the most famous cheer "Sissssss. . . . Boom! . . . Baaahhhhhh." Someone soon discovered that it rhymed with "Rah . . . Rah . . . Rah," and that was the beginning.

Today, cheerleading is a strenuous sport demanding physical fitness and skill. In this age of specialization, it requires long, hard hours of commitment and entails important responsibilities. Cheerleaders are expected, for example, to build school support and spirit for athletic teams, plus set standards of behavior and scholarship for the student body. They also have an obligation to exercise sound judgment at all times. The impression they make must always be a good one. After all, it's a privilege to represent one's school, friends, and community.

These days, being a cheerleader is not easy. Channeling the enthusiasm of others in the proper direction takes someone who is liked and respected and whose behavior, appearance, and attitude are above reproach. It takes a person who can cooperate and communicate with administrators, sponsors, coaches, squad members, students, spirit club members, and fans—upon whom the success of any sports program depends. Not everyone can relate well to a vast number of people. How about you? Maybe you have what it takes to be a cheerleader!

For starters, you've got to be healthy. Cheerleading requires strength and stamina. Spiritleaders are on the go all year long—practicing cheers, writing skits, planning pep rallies as well as attending classes and doing homework. Sometimes they have to cheer for more than one sports team on the same day. If you haven't had a checkup recently, consult your doctor for professional advice about your physical condition and endurance.

Next, be certain you can meet your school's cheerleading qualifications. While qualifications vary from one school to another, the experts at the National Cheerleaders Association (NCA) report that potential spiritleaders should

- Be physically fit.

- Have parental permission to try out, along with permission to attend all practice sessions and games if elected.

- Have a grade point average that meets, or surpasses, the eligibility requirements set for the school's athletic teams, and that reflects your ability to adjust to the demands of extracurricular activities.

- Be friendly, outgoing, cooperative, and courteous.

- Be a school leader with the ability to work well with others.

- Have good verbal skills—the ability to communicate effectively and to listen.

- Have genuine spirit and enthusiasm, and not be reluctant to show that spirit when cheering for your team.

- Have a keen interest in the school's athletic program. Even better, have sports savvy—understand sports rules and regulations.

You need your parents' permission to try out. The permission form in your "tryout pack" will explain the duties and financial obligations of a cheerleader. In your "tryout pack" you may also find a medical release to be signed by a parent and citizenship forms to be completed by your teachers.

- Be well-coordinated and have a distinct sense of rhythm in order to perform routines smoothly and gracefully.

- Have a strong voice with a pleasant quality. (A voice that's high-pitched, whiny, or harsh doesn't go over with a crowd.)

- Have self-control.

- Be aware of the financial responsibilities of a spirit-leader, and be able to provide necessary uniforms, letters, pompons, and megaphone.

- Be able to attend summer cheerleading camp with the squad.

Still, there's more to becoming a cheerleader than meeting the above qualifications. You should have an excellent sense of responsibility. Even then, cheerleading may be more demanding of your time and energy than you realize. Below are obligations the NCA says you can expect if you do become a spiritleader. Make sure you are willing to

- Boost school spirit.

Check that you can attend cheerleading camp with the squad.

- Lead cheers and perform routines at sporting events and pep rallies.

- Promote good sportsmanship among the student body.

- Promote better relationships between schools in your conference.

- Be present and punctual for all practice sessions and games.

- Build a good working relationship with all members of the cheerleading squad.

- Be courteous and friendly to sports teams from other schools.

- Set a good example as a representative of your friends, school, and community.

- Maintain academic grades by participating in class— asking questions, volunteering observations, listening well, and doing homework.

- Have a neat and well-groomed appearance at all times.

• Abide by your school's cheerleading rules and regulations.

If you've never *really* thought about why you want to be a cheerleader, maybe it's time you did. Because cheerleading is so time-consuming, it's important to consider your motives. Chances are, you'll come up with some truly worthwhile reasons for pursuing a position on the squad.

## Get Set

Spring is when most schools select cheerleaders for the following year. Some hold separate tryouts for seventh grade, eighth grade, freshman, junior varsity, and varsity squads.* Check your school's eligibility requirements. Also, find out when and where the training sessions are being conducted by the current cheerleaders. Finally, get in the spirit of things. For a top contender, preparation is a *must*!

---

* With the advent of girls' sports, more and more schools are discovering they have too many events for one squad to cheer. For practical reasons, therefore, they are establishing additional squads at each level. When responsibilities are shared, it is generally the duty of the head cheerleader to designate who cheers when, unless, prior to tryouts, candidates have indicated a preference. Then those with highest tryout scores are assigned their first choice.

There's a lot more to cheerleading than just cheering—much more.

Now's the perfect time to lose weight, if you should, and establish some good eating habits. Whether you are watching your weight or dieting seriously, junk food calories should be the first ones to go. When protein, vitamins, and minerals are in short supply, you may begin to sag. And that's the last thing you want to happen, with all there is to do. To keep strong, plus build stamina, you need a well-balanced diet.

Sometime during the winter, if it's possible, sign up for a dance or gymnastic class. Either is just the thing for developing grace and flexibility and putting you in shape for cheerleading.

Next, study the top cheerleaders. Use the best ones as guides to your technique for the cheers you'll have to perform at tryouts.

Then, each day for sixty minutes follow this plan: To warm up lazy muscles and increase your flexibility, start with the NCA stretching exercises in Chapter 2. If you're thinking about skipping this part, think again. Flexibility is important for an athlete, regardless of the sport. Not only does good flexibility make it easier to perform new skills, but it decreases the risk of serious injury. So loosen up, then go to work perfecting your cheerleading skills. (See Chapters 3, 4, and 7.) Simply wanting to be a cheerleader won't secure you a place on the squad if you aren't good enough. But then the same thing holds true for football or soccer players. It stands to reason that an athlete must have something special to offer in order to earn a spot on the team. So practice, practice, practice!

Next, recruit a friend who is also trying out for cheerleading, or find someone whose knowledge and frankness you appreciate, and ask that he or she watch you carefully. There are times when hearing the whole truth can be painful, but when you're concentrating on becoming a cheerleader, there's no time to be sensitive—or look for an excuse—when your friend has a good point. In this case, complete honesty can serve a real purpose. It will give you a chance to improve your presentation before it goes public.

Now, cheer for your mother, your father, your neighbor, your dog, and the bathroom mirror. (But *never* cheer at school at night without supervision.) If you don't like what you see in the mirror, do something about it. Keep working until you are executing the yells smoothly and have gained confidence in your ability. The more prepared you are, the less uptight you will be as spring tryouts approach.

Pay attention to everything the top cheerleaders do.

Heed the advice of the NCA and practice using your voice properly, or you may come home from sporting events without it. Yell from your diaphragm—the sheet of muscles separating the chest from the abdominal cavity. To avoid damaging your vocal cords do not use your throat. When you shout correctly, you can actually feel your diaphragm pushing the air out—place one hand slightly above your stomach and just a little below your chest and try it.

When cheering, keep your voice in a low, *natural* tone, and simply amplify the sound. (Screaming is guaranteed to turn others off.) Enunciate so that your words are distinguishable and easy to follow, and don't let them run together.

What you wear on tryout day is important. Don't wear sneakers that have seen better days. The NCA suggests that you choose a simple outfit that allows you to move easily, so attention centers on your skill, rather than your clothing. For boys, shorts and an easy-fitting knit sports shirt are appropriate (cut-off jeans are not).

Girls, too, should wear shorts and nice looking T-shirts. They should avoid cut-offs, sloppy T-shirts, halter tops, and jewelry.

Choose a hairstyle that's neat, flattering, and away from the face. It should look natural rather than contrived. Girls with longer hair can pull it back with barrettes, combs, or ribbons—perhaps using the colors of your school.

It's smart to do any experimenting with your hair now, not on your way out the door to tryouts. Also, if you decide what you're going to wear, you can see how everything looks together—while there's still time to make a change. The more comfortable you are with your appearance, the more confident you'll feel when you try out.

Having the right attitude is helpful, too. If you've been unsuccessful at previous cheerleading auditions, try to forget any bad memories still hounding you. Don't let them dampen your spirits. What happened before doesn't have to happen now. People will evaluate the person you are today, not the one you were a year ago. So devote your energy to planning carefully, and stop worrying about losing graciously.

Although the exact process of selecting cheerleaders differs from school to school, schools that share the experience and wisdom the NCA has to offer *hold preliminary tryouts before qualified judges** then have the student body do the final voting. The reason is that today greater emphasis is put on a candidate's cheerleading skills than on one's popularity.

It is helpful to know what judges look for in a cheerleader. The NCA recommends that judges choose well-rounded individuals whose ability, enthusiasm, and appearance make them the finest representatives of their school.

The NCA sets the highest standards around. Therefore, if you're really serious about wanting to be a cheerleader, you'd be wise to rate yourself against their measurements.

• *Ability*—Good, strong motions that flow with the timing and rhythm of the cheer are essential, whether a candidate is performing an original or an established cheer. All motions should be snappy, easy to follow, and presented using proper technique (turn to Chapter 3). More than any other motion, the jump demonstrates spirit. Jumps a candidate may be asked to do are a spread eagle, Herkie,** toe touch, and

---

* The NCA advocates the panel of judges be composed of former cheerleaders (seniors), cheerleader sponsor, and NCA staff members, when available. In choosing the finalists, it is recommended that 50 percent of one's score is based on preliminary tryouts, 25 percent on four teacher evaluations, and 25 percent on a written exam on cheerleading, football, basketball, and soccer.
** Named after the originator, Lawrence R. Herkimer, founder of the National Cheerleaders Association.

Judging the preliminaries.

banana. Judging is based on height, flexibility, form, and grace in the air, together with the smoothness of landing.

• *Enthusiasm*—A good cheerleader radiates spirit and enthusiasm. A smile is catching and therefore an asset in communicating with an audience. (If you're wearing braces, don't worry, you've got plenty of company.) Judges look at the way a candidate projects his or her personality and voice.

• *Appearance*—A teen-ager doesn't have to be fabulous looking to be selected as a spiritleader. But a candidate's weight and height must be in proportion in order to make a positive contribution to one's self-image. A healthy self-image gives a cheerleader more poise and self-assurance. In turn, these characteristics create drawing power, a special power to draw the crowd—only then can one control it in any situation.

## You're On!

You're lucky if you aren't nervous. The truth is it's natural to be scared—even though you've waited for this day a long time. If your heart pounds, your stomach churns, and your knees begin to shake, sharing the worry with a friend sometimes helps release the tension. Or you might try taking a few deep breaths, then urging your body and mind to relax, while you concentrate on your routines. Whatever you do, don't fret about it. Pent-up emotion often creates an explosion of energy when it's released, which can enable you to jump higher, spread your legs wider!

When it's time to audition, plunge right in. Imagine you're cheering for your best friend, or the mirror, while keeping eye contact with the judges. If the thought of doing so makes you gulp, try taking a cue from the NCA by selecting two different spots above the judges and shifting your eye focus (not your head) from one to the other. This will give the impression that you're looking at them.

If you make a mistake, don't panic or make a face. Simply ask the judges if you may begin again and act confident in your ability—whether you are or not. Put enthusiasm in your voice and turn on the spirit with a smile. But don't over-perform. A painted-on smile or a presentation that's too spirited can turn off the judges. Instead, be yourself—even if it's your nervous self—at the very best you can possibly be! And you'll be on your way to making it as a cheerleader.*

Once you have been chosen, in or out of uniform you represent your school. Everything you do—good or bad—reflects upon its image. Those who chose you as a spirit-leader felt that you would make a good impression. And you will, if you

- Are a natural leader by setting a good example.

- Are friendly and courteous to everyone. (If you're stuck-up or act conceited, no one's going to like you for long. So don't get carried away by self-importance.)

- Learn to make others feel important. Look them in the eye and smile as they speak to you. Never interrupt or make sarcastic remarks.

- Keep an open mind. Be willing to admit you're not perfect. When necessary, acknowledge your error and assume responsibility for it.

- Be a sport and teach others to be good sports too by the example you set.

- Have self-control. Always remain calm under stress and try to save your tears for when you're alone.

- Be respectful of administrators, teachers, coaches, players, fans, parents, and other students.

- Be a self-starter. Willingly assume responsibility without being asked, told, or praised. Help when needed, rather than offering an excuse as to why you can't.

---

* There's a sad fact you undoubtedly already know. There are always more students auditioning than there are cheerleading spots available. Consequently, becoming a spiritleader may sound like an impossible dream. Yet it isn't. But you won't know that unless you try out!

Congratulations! You've got what it takes!!

- Take time to understand a problem, then follow it through to completion. When necessary, discuss it with an adult in authority.

- Always look your best. Take pride in your appearance. Be sure your uniform is clean and well-pressed and that you are well-groomed.

- Stay with your squad until the game has ended. Don't eat, drink, or chew gum while on the field or court, or visit with friends or sit with a date during a game.

- Remember, training is important for the athlete. Physical fitness can't be bought. It's dependent upon your daily living habits. This means watching your weight, eating balanced meals, reporting for practice, and getting sufficient rest. There's no place in a cheerleader's life for smoking, drinking, or drugs.

- Do well in school.

- Work at perfecting your routines. Always be coachable.

- Never try to prove how accomplished you are by putting others down. A person who is truly successful doesn't have to do that.

- Smile. Then everyone around you will feel better.

# Stretching into Shape

Always start with warmups. It just isn't fair to expect your body to function at maximum efficiency without some advance notice. Your heart, lungs, and muscles need time to get going. If you make unreasonable demands on your body, you may learn the hard way with pulled muscles and strained ligaments.

Before every practice and game, ward off aches and pains and rev up circulation by always limbering up back, leg, arm, and other muscles that really get a workout in cheerleading. Exercise with the knowledge that a good jump and double stunt require a strong and flexible body. You want to loosen your muscles, not tighten them, and you need to increase their range of motion.

For maximum results, try these stretching exercises developed by the United States Olympic Team. Set aside twenty minutes to do them—twenty-five is even better—and *never* do less than fifteen minutes' worth before practice or a game. Memorize them so you can swing from one to the next without stopping to think. When exercises call for hold, hold your position comfortably, gently stretching, not straining, and count by thousands: "one thousand one, one thousand two, one thousand three . . ." No bouncing is necessary. Each day, gradually increase the number of times you do each exercise.

### The NCA Stretching Exercise Program

## RUNNING

All it takes is a minute or two of jogging to relax the muscles. This can be done anywhere that you can find three square feet of floor.

## ARM CIRCLES

Fully extend arms to the side at shoulder level. Then swing them in circular motions—first to the front ten times, next to the back. Relax, and repeat to stretch your arm and shoulder muscles.

## THE TOE CURL

Sit on the floor with upper body erect, legs together. Creep knees and flex toes toward your chest for eight counts, relax. Grasp calves and repeat. Then grasp ankles and do the same. Last, grasp toes and hold for eight again. With that, you will have stretched the calves, feet, Achilles tendons, muscles behind the knees, hamstrings, and lower back.

## THE HURDLE

Sit on the floor with one leg extended in front of your body, the other bent back with foot arched. Grasp thumbs together, then stretch them over the ankle of extended leg. Next, lean as far back as you can, using the upper part of your body.

## SEAL STRETCH

Lie on the floor, facedown. Push up with arms, keeping hips down while lifting head; hold for five counts. Then shift body position so that you are sitting on your heels. Using hands for balance, raise head up and push shoulders toward the ground. Repeat both parts of this exercise to stretch the small of the back, chest, neck, and shoulder muscles.

## ELEPHANT WALK

Stand with feet, hips, shoulders, and hands all in a straight line. With feet on the floor, stretch the arms and fingertips upward. Now, bend at the waist, place palms of hands on the floor and walk slightly forward, until heels are off the ground. Then try pushing heels to the ground, without permitting them to touch it. This stretches the calf muscles.

## LEG KICKS

Stand parallel to a wall. Then place the hand that is closest to the wall on the wall at shoulder level. Kick outside leg up to the side of your body, keeping toes pointed and leg straight, eight times. Then reverse direction and repeat for eight again to stretch the side muscles and tighten the hips and thighs. Later, try this same exercise without the help of the wall. Instead place your hands on hips.

## KNEE STRETCH

Stand with feet together, hands on knees. Gently push back on the knees and hold for four seconds. Then rotate knees in circular motions from side to side; and push back again to stretch the tendons behind the knees.

## UPPER THIGH STRETCH

Stand with feet slightly apart. Bring right leg up; grasp midsection of right foot with right hand. Touch heel to buttocks, contract buttocks muscles. Then move knee to straight-up-and-down position and pull it back while applying pressure to arch of foot. Hold for eight counts. Relax. Repeat with left leg up.

## BACK BEND

Lie on floor with knees bent at 90-degree angle and feet on the floor, arms at side. Push up with arms and legs to a back bend, keeping legs straight and upper back—not lower back—arched. Arms should be straight.

## SIDE SQUAT

Squat on the floor with right knee bent toward the side, left leg fully extended toward opposite side. For balance, brace with palms or fingertips, and push hips toward the ground to stretch legs. Hold for four counts. Then alternate leg positions and repeat.

## ANKLE AND WRIST ROTATION

While standing, rotate wrists in a circular motion, flexing all parts. Simultaneously rock one ankle, then the other, in the same manner.

## SPLITS

Sit on the floor with legs straddled (straight) and toes pointed. Stretch to a left split for eight counts. Then to a right split for eight more. Relax and repeat to stretch the hips and inside muscles of the legs. (Save this exercise until you can do the splits.)

Athletes should ALWAYS wind down after strenuous exercise by walking for several minutes so that accelerated blood flow to the heart is not reduced too quickly.

# Getting Down to Basics*

Everybody knows good cheerleading skills aren't something you're born with. You *need* to learn them to be a successful cheerleader. Research shows that good skills encourage a crowd to express its enthusiasm; and spirit, in turn, can inspire a team to greater heights!

If you haven't even come close to mastering the skills of cheerleading, don't despair. The mechanics of cheerleading, like algebra and French, can be learned. If you begin with the basics, you can build from there, gradually developing your own unique style. Naturally, you don't want to be a carbon copy of someone else. Still, there are certain fundamentals that help to motivate an audience and enhance your performance.

A cheerleader directing a crowd can be compared to a conductor of a symphony orchestra. Each uses motions that are dynamic and distinct. In both instances, big motions generate big sounds.

To produce the finest results, a cheerleader's gestures should support the words of the cheer and add impact. Important words, such as *go, fight, win*, require strong, well-executed, nonverbal signals to emphasize them. Words of lesser importance need showy, descriptive motions too. Small gestures can't be seen further than the first few rows of the stadium. And most good cheerleaders know that when an audience can't follow a yell, the volume and spirit drop.

---

* If you have been cheering for a while, use this chapter as a guide for sprucing up your skills. You'll be glad you did!

## Hand and Arm Motions

Learn to make a *proper fist,* like the NCA professional pictured. Form a fist, with fingers resting lightly against your palm, but not so lightly that the fist resembles a donut. Position thumb outside fingers, as shown, between the second and third joints. Limp wrists look horrible, so be sure your wrists are *always* straight and firm.

Proper Fist

Next, try using your fists to carry *buckets.* Make a proper fist with each hand. Now, fully extend your arms at natural shoulder level, parallel with the ground. Did you feel them lock in the pocket of your shoulder? If not, extend them again. Arms should be slightly ahead of your body, within your field of vision, when you're looking directly ahead. All set? Turn your fists toward the ground—in position to tote buckets of water. Remember, arms and wrists should be perfectly straight.

Buckets

Candlesticks

To make *candlesticks,* follow directions for proper fists. Then, with a vigorous but smooth motion, fully extend your arms at natural shoulder level—again parallel with the ground. Again, your arms should be straight and slightly in front of the body, within your peripheral vision, when you're looking straight ahead. Then turn fists perpendicular to the ground, as if they were candlesticks about to hold candles.

For *blades,* stand with your arms at your sides. Thrust them overhead to a spot approximately parallel with your ears. Be ouro thoy movo in unioon and otay within your fiold of vioion when you look directly ahead. Arms ought to be straight and of equal distance from your head. Hands should appear to be an extension of the arms, open and flat, like blades, rather than curved or cupped. Your fingers belong together with thumbs in close to the fingers. Wrists should not be broken or bent.

Blades at natural shoulder level and straight up.

Blades, like buckets and candlesticks, may be executed in several positions. For example, on the diagonal or V (as demonstrated on page 25). For other possibilities see the next chapter, or put your imagination to work.

Hands make the most noise when you *clap* with them slightly cupped, rather than flat. When you applaud, get into the habit of keeping fingers together and thumbs in—in a modified blade position. That's how they look best.

To properly *clasp* your hands, first form blades, approximately twelve inches apart. As you bring hands together, thumbs should move away from the forefingers at the point where hands touch so they can clasp opposite hand—without a sound. A clasp should never be a "death grip." If it is, you may find you're losing a beat while you pry your hands apart during a cheer.

Next on the list of motions you want to know: *Tabletops.* Begin by making proper fists. Then place your arms in front of you, with elbows bent, as if they were resting on a table-top. Arms should be level and parallel, not turned out. Your chin ought to be slightly up, as if looking at the fans, not the tabletop.

Clasp

Tabletops

A *diagonal* is easy—just think of the face of a clock. Fully extend your arms on the slant to the two and eight positions. Finish off with blades or proper fists. Either is fine. Just be sure the diagonal is in view.

A variation is a *V*, when you drive your arms overhead—at two and ten on the clock. Whether you combine this motion with blades or proper fists, remember that arm angles must ALWAYS be uniform.

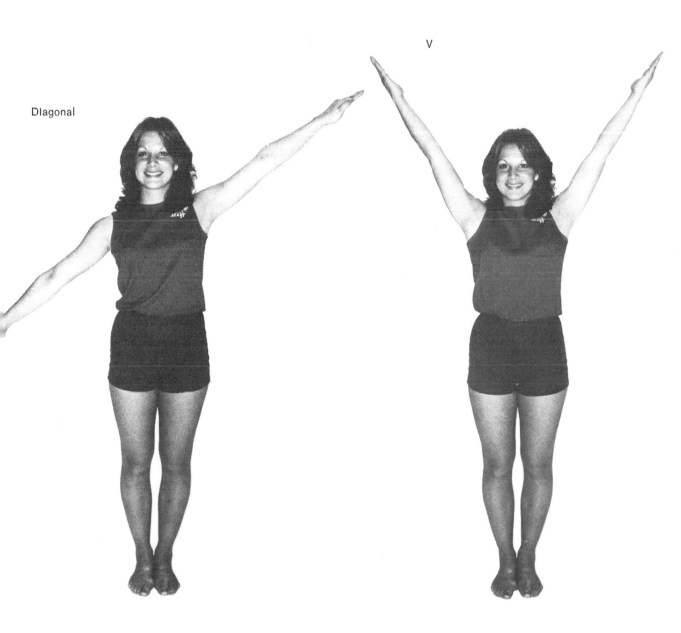

Diagonal

V

To make an *inverted V,* shoot your arms (and proper fists or blades) down to the four and eight. Check that your wrists are firm, arms straight, and arm angles uniform. Finally, be sure you can see the motion.

Now, don't forget to SMILE!

Inverted V

If you really want to look your best—and of course, you do—AVOID

- Thumbs up like a hitchhiker's, or tucked inside the fingers, where they can be sprained easily. And a fist that's too loose really isn't a fist at all.

- Fingers apart.

- Wrists that are bent.

- Arm angles that aren't uniform.

- Flying arms that move about, instead of locking in position.

- Hyperextended arms that are back and out of the range of your peripheral vision. One of the best ways of stopping the motion while your arms are still ahead of your body is by pretending you're cheering with your back to a brick wall.

- Bent arms.

Cheerleaders who are double-jointed should learn to relax their arms when cheering, not tighten or tense them. That's not to say they shouldn't thrust their arms out with a motion that's every bit as demonstrative and firm as the rest of the squad's. But they must locate the point where the arms begin bending and curving inward, and avoid locking them in place. A tip for those with this problem: for good-looking motions, practice in front of the mirror, where you can see what you are doing. This will help you make sure the action is stopped at precisely the right spot.

Lunge . . . to the side

## Foot Notes

Now you're ready to learn the proper way to *lunge*, first to the side, as shown; then, to the front.

When you lunge to the side, the knee of your lunging leg (bent leg) should be directly over your ankle, your foot should be pointing toward the lunge, and your thigh should be as parallel to the ground as possible. Your back leg should be straight, with foot pointing toward the front. (Feet should form a 90-degree angle.) Last, be sure your head is up.

To do a front lunge, bent knee should again be directly over your ankle. The back leg is straight with your foot turned slightly out. Whether you are lunging to the front or the side, the knee should never extend over the ankle, or fall behind it. Nor should both legs ever be bent. The placement of your feet is especially important for stability and balance.

Many cheers incorporate lunges, and many don't. Even when standing straight, you should aim for balance. Slumping wastes energy and doesn't help your appearance. You tire more quickly when your weight isn't properly distributed, since one part of the body or another must shift out of its normal position and compensate for the strain. You should always stand

- With your *feet* parallel and slightly apart, not pointed inward or outward.

- With your *knees* slightly relaxed, not rigid or thrust back.

- With your *hips* under you, not shifted to the side, back, or front.

- With your *abdomen* in.

- With your *chest* held high.

- With your *shoulders* and *arms* cheering free and easy, and your *head* and *chin* centered over your body as you look up at the crowd.

## Jumps

Although it's certainly not the end of the world if you don't have the very best *jump*, don't resign yourself to jumping poorly when there's always something you can, and should, do about it. A good jump is one of the most useful skills of cheerleading. It's the perfect way to spark spirit, add interest to the middle of a cheer, or sustain enthusiasm after a chant is over.

Some cheerleaders seem to have a natural ability to jump well. But the truth is, what it takes to have a super-looking jump is know-how. And what you need to know is here. So limber up and PRACTICE. Make a good jump your top priority.

A good jump is all a matter of timing, lifting, and springing. To help you find the right combination to time the lifting of your arms with the springing of your legs, here are step-by-step directions from the NCA. Surprisingly, though there are many types of jumps, the general approach and the mechanics are the same for all.

- *Approach*—Use the two-step approach to get the most height, since that's what you're after. Start with arms up and out to the side (see photos). Take one step forward, swing both arms down; bring feet together, and . . .

- *Lift*—Lift with the arms, chest, and head, all at the same time. The secret of getting maximum height is using your arms properly. When you lift, pretend you're reaching for the sky and exert a lot of effort. At the same time, keep in mind that you should be looking straight ahead, not up or down. One of the worst things you can do is dip too low. That's hard on the knees, and contrary to what some people think, you don't get the added height.

• *Execution*—Learn to jump off the balls of your feet, making use of the power in your legs. Concentrate on controlling your entire body. Start with pointing your toes—this means arching your feet and stretching them whenever you're in the air. For most jumps legs should be straight and fully extended. Always keep your motions definite; arms straight, fingers together, head up, and back arched. And always hold your stomach in. If you practice in front of a full-length mirror, you'll see a jump looks nicest with top form.

• *Landing*—To look really good, flex your knees, so you land lightly and smoothly—with a bounce on the balls of your feet. Don't land flat-footed, or kick up at the end of a jump. Smile! You want the fans to think you're jumping with effortless ease and that cheerleading is fun!

Herkie—arms out. Herkie jumps are named after their originator, Lawrence R. Herklmer, founder of the National Cheerleaders Association.

## NCA JUMP TECHNIQUE

Approach:   Take one step forward, swing both arms down, bring feet together.

Lift:   Lift with arms, head, and chest; look forward, not down.

Execution:   Point toes; legs should be fully extended and arm motions definite.

Landing:   Land on the balls of feet with knees flexed.

At the beginning, learning to jump can be frustrating, so use a spotter. Ask another person to stand directly behind you and place his or her hands on your waist. When you begin your takeoff, the spotter should lift too. This adds to your momentum. After that, try it again—and again. Then reread this section on jumps before you begin jumping on your own.

Once you've got it, enjoy it! Make the most of your ability to jump by practicing those on the following pages.

## JUMPS

Spread Eagle (arms up)

Banana

Spread Eagle (arms out)

Jumping Jack

Tuck

Cannonball

Bambi

Stag

C-Jump

Back Arch

Herkie—arms at waist.

Herkie—salute.

Split Russian

Toe Touch

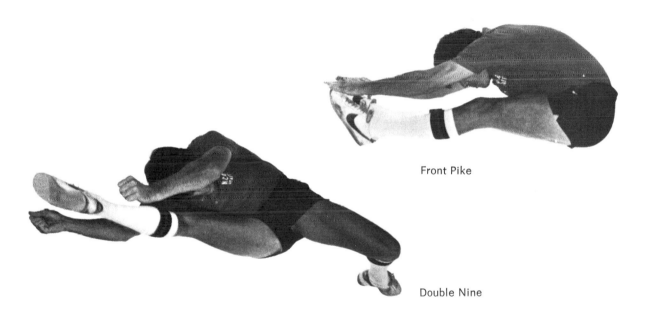

Front Pike

Double Nine

When it's game time, remember these four tips from the NCA.

1. Always jump FACING the crowd.
2. When a jump occurs within a cheer, maintain the rhythm of the cheer by incorporating the jump smoothly. (To do this, you must learn to time the height of the jump with the beat. Later, as a squad, you can work on precision.)
3. After a series of jumps always "break" toward the crowd.
4. Don't do too many continuous jumps. When you tire, you lose both height and precision.

## Splits

Loosen up before you begin working on splits to save your-self the torture of muscles that complain of strain. Then learn the *proper techniques.*

You're sure to be pleased when you can do the splits at the end of a cheer or use them in partner stunts and pyramids. A WARNING: NEVER EXECUTE A JUMP AND LAND INTO THE SPLITS OR YOU MAY TEAR THE MUSCLES IN YOUR LEGS! And always concentrate on relaxing your leg muscles.

With your hands resting on two chairs, straddle with one

leg in front and one in back. Now, gently lower your body to stretch the hamstring and calf muscles. Stop when you feel a burning sensation anywhere in your legs. This means that you have extended the split as far as your muscles will allow. DO NOT BOUNCE. Simply stretch, as illustrated. Repeat the same procedure for several weeks. As your flexibility increases, so will the width of your splits, but meanwhile be patient. It takes many weeks to stretch into a split, and that's that. Cheerleaders who have tried to find a shortcut to the process are the first to share their pulled-muscle stories.

So, remove the chairs and practice gradually sliding into a split, keeping your hands and arms in position to aid in bracing if you begin to fall. Ease on down to the ground with one leg in front; then always do the same with the other. In posi-

Now, kneel on one knee and form a ninety-degree angle with the other, as shown. Push your hips forward, stretching the hamstring, using both hands for balance. Once the hamstrings are stretched, extend the lower leg and again press

tion, toes should be pointed as you sit on the floor. Upper torso ought to be perpendicular to your legs, somewhat like an inverted letter *T*.

down to stretch the calf. Alternating front legs, continue this process for a few weeks. By then, your splits will be nearly perfect.

The Chinese splits . . . with both legs fully extended to the side!

Next, try this: just step forward into a kneeling position and slide your front foot forward. As your legs move apart, your hands should brace against the floor for support.

**To recover a standing position,** or get out of the splits, try bending both knees and bringing both feet toward your body. Cross your back leg over your front knee, then shift weight forward onto your front foot as you stand. Your back foot should slide into a *semi-third position*.

# Cheering with the NCA*

A cheer is easiest to learn when there's someone who can guide you through the movements and offer constructive help. Remember, once you've mastered each routine, polish it and make it look like fun!

(*Note:* Many of the positions illustrated in this chapter can be used in different sequence when you make up a new shout, or when you use the cheers in Chapter 8.)

---

* Seasoned cheerleaders can put the cheers in this chapter into their game plans.

Starting Position      Offense      Defense

Defense      At . . .      Tack!

Push 'Em

Back

Offense

1. Starting position.
2. Extend arms up above head.
3. Bring fists down on tabletops with elbows bent.
4. Punch fists out and cross right fist over left.
5. Lunge forward on left foot and extend arms with palms down.
6. Step forward on right foot and extend arms at sides.
7. Extend arms straight above head.
8. Bring fisted arms down in front of thighs.
9. Lunge forward on right foot and extend arms with palms down.

**DEFENSE**
*(a football cheer)*
D-E-F-E-N-S-E
Hit 'Em Right
Hold 'Em Tight
Vic-to-ry

Starting Position

D

N

S

E

E                              F                              E

1. Starting position.
2. Slap hands on the floor.
3. Lunge left, punch right fist out in front, left fist on hip.
4. In same lunge position, swing right fist toward the left. Left hand on hip.
5. Bring feet together, punch both fists out.
6. Step back on right foot, punch left fist out in front, right elbow bent.
7. Bring feet together, punch both fists out in front.
8. Widen stance, fisted arms extended out to sides.

*(continued on next page)*

Hit 'Em                    Right

To-                                    Ry!

Hold 'Em                Tight                Vic-

9. Step back on right foot, punch left fist out in front, right elbow bent.
10. Bring feet together, punch both fists out.
11. Cross arms in front, grasp elbows.
12. Clasp hands in front.
13. Slap thighs.
14. Widen stance, arms fisted and extended out to sides.
15. Step forward on right foot, bring blades up.

**OFFENSE**
*(a basketball cheer)*
O-F-F-E-N-S-E
Shoot It Right
Win Tonight
Vic-to-ry

Starting Position

O

N

S

E

F                        F                        E

1. Starting position.
2. Punch fists down, flex knees slightly.
3. Step out on right foot, point toes. Bring right fist back, punch left fist out.
4. Put right foot down, punch both fists forward.
5. Turn to side. Punch left fist out. Right fist up. Point right toe.
6. Bring feet together, cross fists over head.
7. Thrust fisted hands up in V.
8. Flex knees, fists on hips.

*(continued on next page)*

Shoot      It      Right

Vic-      To-      Ry!

Win                         To-                         Night

9.   Step out on left foot, point toe, bring left fist back, punch
     right fist out.
10.  Bring feet together. Tabletops.
11.  Thrust fists out to sides.
12.  Inverted V with fists.
13.  Tabletops.
14.  V with fists.
15.  Fists at sides, left toe pointed.
16.  Tabletops. Flex right knee.
17.  V with fists.

## A Pompon Routine

When a squad performs, pompons add intensity to the cheer. For this flair, female cheerleaders may want to try the following pompon routine to a tune with a catchy beat.

After you and your squad have this down pat, sport it at half time for entertainment. A pompon routine isn't meant to fire up fans during a game, but it's a nice change of pace and adds color and pizzazz to intermission.

The National Cheerleaders Association tells you how to polish your performance: For starters, punch and snap all motions into position. Use the power in your arms to stop the action at a precise point. Hyperextension will make motions look loose, and, if you simply set your arms in place, your motions won't appear definite.

Kicks should be uniform and perfect. This means total body control is essential. Be sure that your arms don't leave your hips in the middle of a kick and that your back doesn't bend into the kick. Always keep an erect, upright posture. Although kicks can be tiring, it's important that your kicking leg is always straight and firm. Don't allow your knee to bend and, equally important, keep toes pointed.

Remember to smile, even at the highest point of a kick. So that all kicks are uniform, a squad must agree on a desired height. This means some cheerleaders may have to lower their kicks, while others will have to work to increase their height.

Head motions can be used for emphasis or simply as a single beat. When turning, keep your eyes focused on the audience until the last split second, then hurriedly whip your head and reestablish direct eye contact. Make sure your face reflects your enthusiasm all along. Pompon routines are fun!

1    2    3

REPEAT STEPS 1–8

7    8    9

---

* Pompons are not pictured, so motions can be better seen.

4                                    5                                    6

1.  Starting position. Hands on hips.
2.  Bend arms at elbows. Right knee also slightly bent.
3.  Punch arms in a V.
4.  Bend arms at elbows. Right knee slightly bent.
5.  Punch arms in a T shape.
6.  Bend arms at elbows. Right knee slightly bent.
7.  Punch arms out in an inverted V.
8.  Step out on right foot. Bend arms right over left. Snap. Repeat back-and-forth motion four counts.

    Repeat steps 1–8.

9.  Raise right leg and bend right arm.

*(continued on next page)*

10

11

12

18

19

20

| 13 | 14 | 15 | 16 | 17 |

10. Punch right fist out as you move to the right.
11. Switch movement to the left. Bend left arm and left leg.
12. Punch left arm out. Right arm on hip.
13. Bring both feet together. Fists directly in front of thighs.
14. Point left toe. Punch right arm out in front. Left arm behind.
15. Bring both feet together. Fists directly in front of thigh.
16. Point right toe. Punch left arm in front. Right arm in back.
17. Bring both feet together. Fists directly in front of thighs.
18. Place fists on hips with feet together.
19. Kick the left leg behind, bending at the knee. Fists on hips.
20. Kick the left leg straight up.

*(continued on next page)*

**21**

**22**

**23**

**27**

**28**

**29**

24                                    25                                    26

21.  Repeat step 19, kicking right leg behind, bending at the knee. Fists on hips.
22.  Repeat step 20, but kick right leg straight up.
23.  Put fists in front of thighs. Left toe slightly up.
24.  Hop on left leg facing left. Bring right leg up with arms out in front.
25.  Legs apart facing front. Arms fisted in a T.
26.  Hop with feet together. Arms in inverted V.
27.  With circular motion bring arms across thighs.
28.  Crossing in front and traveling up—all the way to . . .
29.  High V, ending the routine.

Sooner or later, you're going to want to make up a pompon routine of your own. When the time comes, first select your music, then dream up a variety of actions.

With all the latest hits to choose from, and many from the past, it's sometimes difficult to decide which music is best for a routine. To help make up your mind, here are some questions you should ask yourself before making that decision:

- Is the music appropriate for the group and the game?

- Does the beat set a snappy pace that everyone can comfortably follow? Or is it much too fast, or too slow?

- Does the music need lyrics?

- Is the arrangement too long or too short? It should have a playing time of less than three minutes.

- If live music is to be used, is the piece within the capabilities of the band?

A suitable piece of music has three characteristics:
1.  It's dynamic and exciting.
2.  It varies in tempo, meter, and tone.
3.  It has a strong, definite beat.

Be wary of any tune that's overly repetitious. While some repetition is acceptable, too much can make a routine drag. Furthermore, it is difficult to be creative when measures are repeated.

All routines should have

- A definite beginning and definite ending.

- Balanced arm and leg movements that work together.

- A variety of steps within each spiritleader's capacity to perform.

- Audience appeal.

When you're making up a routine, everything goes—as long as it is in harmony with the music and part of a fitting presentation. For maximum effect, however, all steps must be perfected and the squad must always be in unison, with spacing maintained throughout the production.

Always give yourself plenty of room to work. Begin a routine away from the audience, then move toward it, using a series of balanced formations. A routine should always end closer to the crowd than it began. Here are some tips from the NCA:

- Use BIG, showy movements.

- Look at your crowd.

- Act confident.

- Keep smiling!

*Hint:* To keep pompons looking fresh, carry them to and from school in a plastic bag.

# Cheering with a Partner, and Sometimes Three or Four

Partner stunts and pyramids are two of the most dazzling new ways to brighten your routines. These are crowd pleasers that build momentum and maintain intensity, plus they add to the appearance and effectiveness of a group when used properly. They are also much easier to perform than you may think. That's not to suggest they don't demand balance, timing, and coordination, however. Because they do!

When cheerleaders find even the most elementary double stunts awkward to perfect, it's most often because the partners haven't worked together enough to know how to balance and counterbalance each other's weight. Partner stunts require that partners have complete confidence in one another's ability and an understanding of the four basic principles of double stunts. Here are the facts the NCA feels you should know *before* you attempt a partner stunt:

- The base must be in a correct base position.

- The base must utilize his or her strength points.

- Both base and partner must balance and counterbalance their weights correctly.

- Both base and partner must give total effort and concentration to the stunt. If either is distracted, the stunt will surely fail.

## Words to Add to Your Cheerleading Vocabulary

In this case what you don't know *can* hurt you. Painlessly increase your vocabulary by becoming familiar with these terms:

BASE: The bottom person in a double stunt or pyramid. The base is the holding or lifting partner, therefore he or she must be strong.

BRACE: Those cheerleaders who support other cheerleaders, who depend upon them for balance.

INTERLOCK: The proper way of using the hands and arms to form the outline of a pyramid—palm to palm, palm to top of the hand, palm to forearm, fingertip to fingertip. Cheerleaders should *never* hold hands when building a pyramid.

LEG LIFTS: Those cheerleaders who support other cheerleaders by holding their legs.

LEG LIFT STAND: The partner who stands on leg lift. To avoid injury, partner should mount leg left on thigh strength point, *never* on the knee. Base should support the leg lift by holding one inch above the ankle.

PARTNER: The top person in a partner stunt or pyramid.

PARTNER STUNTS: Also called DOUBLE STUNTS and used to build pyramids.

POST: A center point from which a pyramid expands.

PYRAMID: A combination of partner stunts having various forms of symmetry.

SPOTTER: A person who watches a stunt and helps build it and take it down as safely as possible.

SUPPORTIVE PEOPLE: Squad members who are assigned the task of helping everyone else get into position. They generally have the least difficult stunt to perform.

## THE BASE POSITIONS

## THE STRENGTH POINTS
*(See arrows)*

## Partner Stunts

The NCA's philosophy of SAFETY FIRST is important when learning and executing partner stunts.

For safety's sake, a spotter is always needed to help support a stunt, until the partners feel confident they can perform it safely on their own.

A spotter may stand in front, back, or at the side of the base, wherever he or she can best aid in lifting, then holding the partner, until the stunt looks balanced and secure. For boy-girl stunts, the spotter generally concentrates on spotting the shoulder area and helps in lifting by holding the outside arm of the mounter. To be sure, if any stunt is especially difficult, it's advisable to have two spotters. In any case, it's always the spotter's job to remain alert and help break the fall of the partner should a stunt collapse.

Naturally, partners should perfect a stunt and know they can execute it well before performing it in public. Even then, it should be presented only at an appropriate time. (See Chapter 8.)

Partner stunts should be learned in an orderly fashion, according to their degree of difficulty. On the pages that follow, do not skip from one partner stunt to the next until you have mastered one. To be on the safe side, pay special attention to mounting and dismounting techniques.

PONY MOUNT
1. Base Position Two
2. Partner Position—left hand on Base's shoulder, right hand in middle of Base's back
3. Partner jumps on Base in sitting position, feet together behind Base
4. DISMOUNT—Partner returns hands to mounting position, then pushes off with right hand on Base's back
5. SPOT—should be done from behind the stunt

## PARTNER STUNTS

COWBOY
1. Base Position Two
2. Partner Position—same as for Pony Mount
3. Partner jumps on Base in sitting position
4. Partner raises right hand, lowers right foot
5. Base raises left hand, places right hand on top Partner's right foot
6. DISMOUNT—Partner returns hands to mounting position, then pushes off with hand on Base's back
7. SPOT—should be done from behind the stunt

## L-CATCH

1. Base Position One
2. Partner Position—kneels with left knee on Base's bent knee
3. Partner lifts right leg
4. Base catches Partner's right ankle

## SIDE THIGH STAND

1. Base Position One
2. Partner Position—step up on Base's thigh with inside foot
3. Base holds Partner at waist, then slides hand down to thigh for added support as . . .
4. Partner steps up with second leg
5. DISMOUNT—Partner jumps forward
6. SPOT—Base spots by holding Partner at waist. If used, added spotters stand to the side and behind the stunt.

## SIDE THIGH SIT
1. Base Position One
2. Partner Position—stands at side of Base's bent leg. One hand on shoulder, one hand at waist
3. Base puts hand around Partner's waist
4. Partner jumps on Base's thigh in a kneeling position
5. DISMOUNT—Base brings straight leg to lunged leg and "pops" Partner off to the side
6. SPOT—same as side thigh stand

SIDE THIGH STAG
1. Base Position One
2. Partner Position—right knee bent on thigh strength point
3. Partner mounts Base as described in Side Thigh Stand
4. Partner raises outside front foot into a "stag" position
5. Base puts fisted arm around Partner's left thigh
6. DISMOUNT—same as for Side Thigh Stand
7. SPOT—same as for Side Thigh Stand

SIDE THIGH WITH LEG HITCHED
Variation of Side Thigh Stag with outside knee hitched forward.

## SIDE THIGH ARABESQUE

1. Base Position One
2. Partner mounts Base as described in Side Thigh Stand
3. Partner lifts outside leg and leans slightly forward with arms fully extended
4. Base holds Partner's inside leg at thigh
5. DISMOUNT—Partner jumps forward
6. SPOT—Base spots by holding Partner at waist

## SIDE THIGH "L" STAND

1. Base Position One
2. Partner mounts Base as described in Side Thigh Stand
3. Base holds Partner at thigh with right hand
4. Base lifts Partner's inside leg at the ankle with left hand overhead
5. DISMOUNT—Base lowers Partner's leg to Side Thigh Stand position. Dismount same as Side Thigh Stand
6. SPOT—same as Side Thigh Stand

DOUBLE SIDE CATCH
1. Base Position One (legs may be spread slightly farther than shoulder width)
2. Both Partners simultaneously jump onto Base's thighs (as explained in Side Thigh Sit)
3. DISMOUNT—same as for Side Thigh Sit
4. SPOT—same as for Side Thigh Sit
5. Variation Double Side Stand— Partners step onto Base's thighs, inside foot first. A HINT: Partners should step as high on Base's thighs as possible. Base holds near top of Partners' thighs.

COUNTERBALANCE
1. Base Position One
2. Base and Partner face each other, interlocking forearms
3. Base leans back into a sitting position
4. Partner steps on Base's thighs and leans back to "counterbalance" their weight. A WORD OF WARNING: Neither should pull too hard backwards. It's helpful to "ease" into this stunt until balance is gained. DO NOT JUMP INTO IT!
5. DISMOUNT—Base straightens up and Partner jumps a little back and down.
6. SPOT—behind Base and behind Partner

SHOULDER SIT
1. Partner stands in front of Base
2. Base holds Partner's waist
3. Partner bounces and jumps up
4. Base raises Partner as she jumps and places her on his shoulder
5. Base holds Partner with one arm over her thigh
6. Partner locks both legs together and hooks feet around Base's back for stability
7. DISMOUNT—Partner jumps down with Base holding waist
8. SPOT—One person may spot the back of the stunt, another the side where Partner is jumping up

## SHOULDER SIT FRONT ANGLE

1-6. Same as Shoulder Sit
  7. Partner extends both arms to sides, bends left knee across Base's thigh, and extends right leg to the back

## SHOULDER STRADDLE

1. Base holds Partner at waist
2. Base and Partner both dip; as Partner jumps, Base extends the jumps so that Partner can straddle his head
3. Partner then locks feet behind Base for support

DISMOUNT—PIKE DISMOUNT
1. Base and Partner hold hands
2. Base dips and extends his arms, pushing up as Partner extends her arms pushing down
3. Partner pulls up legs parallel to the ground
4. Base holds Partner's arms all the way down

DISMOUNT—REAR TWIST
DISMOUNT
1. Base and Partner hold hands
2. Base pushes arms up as Partner jumps down
3. Base holds Partner's arms all the way down

## TENSION DROP

1. Base and Partner do a Shoulder Stand
2. Base leans over, keeping body straight. Partner DOES NOT lean over
3. Partner jumps off and forward from Base
4. Both Base and Partner do forward rolls, simultaneously
5. SPOT—same as for Shoulder Stand

## SHOULDER STAND

1. Base Position One
2. Partner stands to Base's lunged side and shakes hands with Base right to right, left to left
3. Base pulls Partner up, Partner steps up with right foot on Base's lunged thigh, left foot on Base's left shoulder, right foot on Base's right shoulder
4. Base lets go of Partner's hands, one at a time. THIS IS IMPORTANT!
5. Partner straightens up and looks straight ahead
6. Base holds Partner's upper calves
7. DISMOUNT—Base reaches for Partner's hands, one at a time. THIS IS IMPORTANT!
8. Partner jumps down as Base holds her hands—ALL THE WAY DOWN!
9. SPOT from front and back

## HIGH BIRD

1. Partner steps toward Base
2. Base grasps Partner's thigh bones —palms together
3. Partner jumps at a 60 degree angle, over Base's head
4. Base lifts Partner over his head
5. Partner has head up, back arched, legs and feet together, and toes pointed
6. DISMOUNT—reverse the mount
7. SPOT—Spotter should stand behind Base and to the side

## BUTTERFLY

1. Base places palms together on Partner's bottom
2. Base tilts Partner to vertical position, balancing her on one hand, counterbalancing with other
3. Partner balances herself by placing her nearest arm on Base's shoulder
4. Partner stags her top leg
5. DISMOUNT—reverse of mount
6. SPOT—behind and to back side of stunt

84

BUTT BIRD
1. Base places palms together on Partner's bottom
2. Partner dips and jumps up and back while holding Base's wrists
3. Base lifts Partner as she jumps and holds her in an arched position over head
4. DISMOUNT—Partner clasps Base's wrists, lifts her legs back over her head, and does a suspended back roll. CAUTION: Partner MUST release grasp before she completes suspended back roll to prevent injury to Base's back

BACK ARCH
1. Partner stands on one foot to side of Base
2. Base places one hand in the small of Partner's back, the other on Partner's ankle
3. Partner dips and jumps up and back
4. Base presses Partner up with his hand under her back—to an arched position
5. Partner straightens out bent leg and forms "stag" position
6. Partner lets head and arms hang down
7. Base extends opposite arm
8. Partner turns to handstand position, leg stagged
9. Base extends right arm
10. DISMOUNT—Partner dismounts to Base's left

## HIGH CHAIR

1. Base puts one hand under Partner's seat, one hand around Partner's ankle
2. Partner dips and jumps straight up as Base lifts Partner
3. DISMOUNT—Base tosses Partner up. Partner falls into a cradle position
4. SPOT—from the side of the stunt and from the rear

## CHEEK TO CHEEK

1. Partner jumps and straddles Base's chest
2. Base dips and swings Partner upward to a "headstand" position. Helpful Hint: Partner should keep in a tuck position until Base has swung her up over his head
3. DISMOUNT—Partner "pikes" and Base brings her down
4. SPOT—from behind the base

**ARM TO ARM**
1. Partner faces Base
2. Base Position Three (front lunge)
3. Partner puts one foot on Base's lunged thigh
4. Base and Partner rock back, then forward. As they rock forward, Partner pushes off Base's knee and lifts hips, tucks head, and finally extends body upward
5. DISMOUNT—same as for Cheek to Cheek
6. SPOT—from behind the base

T-LIFT
1. Partner stands to side and slightly in front of Base
2. Partner steps on right foot, then kicks left leg up and straightens out while she leans back, straightening entire body
3. As Partner steps forward and kicks, Base places right hand behind Partner's lower neck and also catches Partner's extended left leg
4. Base then sweeps Partner up in a "T" position
5. HELPFUL HINT—Partner should not bend at the waist as she kicks up. Instead should lean back as Base bends and pushes up—using legs for added power
6. DISMOUNT—to a cradle
7. SPOT—in front and back of stunt

**HIGH STAG**

1. Partner lifts one leg and stands in arabesque position
2. Base holds Partner's upper waist and thigh
3. Partner dips with opposite leg and jumps; as Partner jumps
4. Base presses Partner over his head
5. DISMOUNT—Base lowers Partner
6. SPOT—should stand in front of the stunt

## STRADDLE PRESS
1. Base and Partner perform a shoulder straddle
2. Base places hands under Partner's thighs and pushes her up over his head
3. Partner is in somewhat seated position—legs extended
4. DISMOUNT—Base lowers Partner —spotting at the waist

## FRONT SKATE
1. Partner stands to side of base
2. Base and Partner shake hands, right to right, left to left
3. Partner steps toward, yet slightly behind Base, left foot, right foot, then kicks up with left foot
4. As Base dips down so when Partner kicks up she can straighten and lock her arms above Base's shoulder
5. Base presses with his legs, fully extending arms, so both Base and Partner can assume a vertical position
6. DISMOUNT—Partner turns to left, dismounting on side of Base. As Partner turns, Base spins her hands so that both end up backing forward
7. SPOT—front and back of stunt

POWER SKATE
1. Partner stands behind Base and steps up on Base's calf
2. As Partner steps, Base dips and lifts
3. Base presses with his legs, fully extending his arms so that both Partner and Base assume a vertical position
4. DISMOUNT—same as for Front Skate
5. SPOT—front and back of stunt

SPLIT CATCH
1. Base stands behind Partner and holds on to her waist
2. Partner and Base dip
3. Partner jumps as high as possible into the splits (preferably side split)
4. As Partner jumps, Base thrusts Partner as high as possible, releasing his grip at waist and catching Partner in splits under her thighs for balance. Hint: As Partner jumps she should not look down. Base should look at Partner and not push her forward
5. SPOT—in front and back of stunt

SAILOR
1. Base and Partner start as illustrated
2. Base lifts Partner as Partner keeps body firm
3. Base interlocks Partner's left arm and supports her right leg as he lowers her
4. Partner salutes

FRED ASTAIRE
1. Base and Partner stand as illustrated
2. Partner and Base dip
3. Partner jumps as high as possible
4. Base thrusts Partner upward
5. Partner extends right leg up, bends left knee, and places foot against right leg
6. Partner then brings legs together
7. Base shifts weight to side and supports Partner with raised arms

8. DISMOUNT—Partner jumps down, legs together

STAR LIFT
1. Base and Partner stand as illustrated
2. Base uses power in legs to lift Partner
3. Partner extends both arms in vertical position, legs in corresponding position
4. DISMOUNT—Partner brings legs together, dismounts same as Fred Astaire

NEEDLE LIFT

1. Base and Partner start as illustrated
2. Both Base and Partner dip
3. As Partner jumps up
4. Base uses power in legs and arms to bring Partner to vertical position
5. Partner extends right leg toward the sky, bends left leg, and places it against right thigh
6. Base extends right arm and supports Partner's thigh. Base extends left arm parallel with ground for added balance.
7. DISMOUNT—same as Star Lift

ARM STAND
1. Base and Partner stand as illustrated, interlocking arms, with Base's arms on inside
2. Base lunges to the front
3. Partner places foot on Base's thigh
4. Both rock toward the Partner rather than toward the Base
5. Partner pushes off Base's thigh, lifts hips, and extends legs, executing handstand above Base
6. Base balances the Partner and maintains vertical position
7. DISMOUNT—Partner "pikes" at the waist
8. SPOT—front and behind the stunt

## Pyramids

Pyramids are combinations of double stunts with various forms of symmetry. Skilled cheerleaders effectively incorporate them into introductions, cheers, and chants.

There are many different types of pyramids: *Braced pyramids* are generally vertical in form, and can support more weight than any other type. They are so named because one cheerleader is braced, or securely held in place by another. (For an example, see page 103.) *Split* pyramids are the most spectacular looking because one or more people do splits in it. Accordingly, this type of pyramid is the most dangerous to perform, unless good spotting and lifting techniques are used. (The "splitter" should ALWAYS hold one hand of the base.) *Staircase pyramids* resemble steps. (See page 104.) They are relatively simple to build, because they are usually made up of basic double stunts. But easiest of all to erect are *Double-stunt pyramids*. They expand from a post, or center person (as on page 106), and are always balanced with the same partner stunt. *Triangle pyramids* are also built from the post; however, as the name implies, they form a triangle, with the person farthest from the ground at top center. *Fan pyramids* fan up or down from the post and lean out from the

sides (as on page 107). They must be balanced to look good.

Cheerleaders are busily incorporating more and more pyramids into their cheers, but there is a growing concern among state high school associations, some of which have banned pyramids they consider "ultra-hazardous." The National Cheerleaders Association believes that there is a place for pyramids in cheerleading but that certain safety standards for building and dismounting are essential to reduce the likelihood of injury. Toward that end before you try *any* new ideas, the NCA encourages you to

- Design your pyramid on paper, using the most basic partner stunts when learning to build pyramids, and later graduating to those your squad can execute effectively.

- Decide how to mount safely into your pyramid. Determine which double stunt is most difficult. Those partners with the most difficult stunt should get into position first, with supportive people acting as spotters. Mount into the highest of pyramids using shoulder straddles and shoulder stands to reach the top position.

- Organize the spotting of mounts.

- Decide on the best dismounting procedure. There are several choices: A section of the pyramid can dismount and attract the fans by jumping, which would distract the audience's attention from those cheerleaders who are dismounting from the most difficult positions; or the entire squad can perform a tension drop as described on pages 82 and 83.

- Organize the spotting of your dismount.

When your squad is ready to practice pyramids, every cheerleader should

- Use a spotter always.

- Concentrate on what you are doing, so the pyramid can be constructed with competence and rhythm.

- Think about focusing on the crowd and projecting your voice.

- Hold a constructed pyramid at least three full counts. After that, supportive people should return to their spotting positions and help everyone down.

## PYRAMIDS FOR SPIRITLEADERS

# Tumbling

Gymnastics is not designed only for athletes who have the dedication and perseverance to compete in the Olympics. For the cheerleader, too, gymnastics can be *fun* and challenging, but only when a safe set of performing and spotting techniques are used. If the idea of tumbling sounds appealing, warm up. Below are the how-tos, along with some helpful hints from the NCA:

- Before beginning, visualize the stunt from start to finish.

- Approach all stunts positively.

- When attempting a new stunt, use two spotters who are knowledgeable tumblers.

- Start slowly. Later you can perform the stunt at a comfortable speed.

## TUMBLING

BASIC FORWARD ROLL—Stand with knees and ankles together. Tuck head, put chin between knees, and push off the balls of the feet, executing a forward roll. Roll on the upper portion of back and shoulders, so momentum carries you forward into your original position. Hint: Don't cross knees or ankles, or overflip and land on either the middle section or small portion of your back. SPOT: Spotter places one hand under tumbler's hips and tucks her head, to help execute the stunt.

THE CARTWHEEL—Turn body slightly to the side and kick right foot up as you lean forward and place left hand on the floor. Next, kick both legs off the ground, so that you are in a handstand straddle. Continue rotating, placing front foot on the floor and pushing off with the hands. For the nicest form: Arms and legs must be fully extended, toes pointed. Last hand on the floor should have fingertips pointing toward the opposite hand. This helps achieve a stronger push-off. Hips should be firm and vertical with head and hands. And one more thing: Don't bend at the waist. SPOT: Spotter places inverted hand on the tumbler's front hip, the other on opposite hip. As tumbler executes the stunt, spotter uses own legs for leverage and keeps the performer from collapsing by lifting her body.

THE ROUND-OFF—Turn slightly to the side, as if you were going to do a cartwheel. Begin cartwheel motion. When feet are directly overhead, bring them together. Then make a quarter turn with the hips and snap feet down simultaneously. Land on the balls of your feet, and finish in an upright standing position, with hands up. The gymnast turns 180 degrees from original starting position when doing a well-executed round-off. SPOT: At the waist from the side.

FRONT WALKOVER—To begin the front walkover, both hands are placed on the floor side by side, a shoulder distance apart. The arms should be straight, the head up. Kick to a handstand, keeping feet apart. Then continue over, finishing upright, one foot in front of the other, landing individually. Head should remain back, and the back should be arched throughout the stunt. SPOT: The spotter's hand closest to the tumbler should be inverted and placed on the tumbler's upper arm. The other hand should be used to spot the back. Note: Most cheerleaders find it easier to use a running walkover. Done this way it is quicker and more exciting to watch, thanks to the body's momentum.

TENSICA—Begin the tensica like a cartwheel. But when legs and hips are overhead, twist the hips a quarter turn back so you finish with feet apart, body erect. SPOT: Just as you would the front walkover.

THE BACK WALKOVER—Lean backward as far as possible, extend arms, and look toward the ground. Lift one leg, keeping it extended, and allow it to rotate over you—this increases the backward arch and gives you momentum to complete a back handstand (legs split) and return to a standing position. SPOT: Spotter should spot the tumbler's back and assist in the lifting of legs (up and over).

Preparation for THE BACK HAND-SPRING. Sit back as if you were about to sit in a chair, rather than on a spotter's hands; as you do so let arms swing to side. Torso should be leaning slightly back so that a feeling of imbalance will occur. Knees should be over the ankles or slightly behind them, the waist should be slightly behind the hips. Spotter kneels on one knee with his forearm and hand above his knee to act as a chair. A Word of Warning: If tumbler sits on spotter's knee with shoulders tilted forward, backspring will be poor—resulting in an up-down motion rather than a sit, jump up, and throw-back motion. Therefore, the spotter should grasp the tumbler's shoulder as she sits and pull her shoulders back. Next, jump up as high as possible, swinging the arms upward and jumping off both feet. At the same time tilt the head back. Don't let the head or shoulders bend forward or the eyes look down before you jump. Instead look forward, then up. Now continue the stunt by throwing the arms and head forcefully back. Keep eyes open, place both hands on the floor, arms straight, as if in a handstand position. Last, snap the feet simultaneously to the floor and finish in an upright position —standing on the balls of your feet with hands up.

THE BACK HANDSPRING—Note: The handspring should travel the length of the performer's body when arms are extended. When a shorter distance is traveled, it is generally because the performer leaned forward with the shoulders or tilted the head and eye downward. Also, the performer must jump up in order to have time to rotate and throw-back. Again, be sure to throw the arms and head back as far as possible and keep the eyes open throughout the stunt.

Spotting Aerial Cartwheel

Aerial Cartwheel

AERIALS—A tremendous thrust of the arms and legs is required. Head must be back at all times.

Spotting Aerial Walkover

Aerial Walkover

Standing Back Flip

# Putting Your Skills to Work

No doubt about it—to be a top cheerleader you have to relate well to the crowd. How you relate is just as important as how you cheer and what you say. The fans have something you want—an indispensable show of spirit they can contribute to an entire team's effort. To help you go over big with the crowd, the NCA recommends their proven techniques.

## Spirit

Getting a crowd to shout with you isn't easy, unless you have *genuine* spirit and enthusiasm and aren't afraid to show that spirit when cheering for your team!

People respond to the feelings you transmit. You can't wear a fake smile and feign enthusiasm and expect to arouse excitement in anyone. When you aren't enthusiastic, a crowd won't be very enthusiastic about yelling with you. So put spirit into your voice and use your facial expression to be sure the messages you're sending out are right. Smile and let the fans know you love what you're doing. When you yell, "The Falcons have Go-o-o-o-o-o-o power!" cheer as if you're sure they do. Never do a chant or a cheer in just one tone. Learn to make the most of your expression and literally let your voice yell for you.

This doesn't mean you should scream. There's a big difference between yelling and screaming. Screaming is hard on your vocal cords and on other people's ears. It's also a sure-fire way of turning off your listeners. Even when the fans are

The vibes are right!

seemingly so unspirited that you feel like screaming, don't scold the crowd. The pleasure of doing so will be small compared with the resentment it will invariably incur. If you're ever tempted to shout, ''Okay, all you stupid people up there, *yell!*'' count to ten. Smile. Then, the NCA suggests, you encourage the fans with, ''Hey, you're doing great, but let's hear it a little louder this time.'' You'll be headed in the right direction.

## Eye Contact

Good cheerleaders know it's nearly impossible to hold the interest of an audience while looking at the ground, to the side, or at the other cheerleaders, watching for cues to what they should be doing. When you are unsure of yourself, it shows, and attention is diverted from the cheer itself. Direct eye contact keeps spectators tuned in to what you're saying.

The next time you're cheering, check that you aren't hiding your face with your motions. Be sure you set your sights on the crowd, rather than letting your eyes drift around. Sometimes, when a cheerleader is scared and nervous, there's a tendency to look bug-eyed. If this is a problem of yours, try relaxing and looking like you're having a good time. Looking at cheerleaders whose eyes appear to be jumping out of their heads is an instant turnoff.

## Entrance

Keep in mind how important first impressions really are. All it takes is a few, fast minutes for people to form an impression of you and your squad, which could affect your rapport with the fans. Be certain the first impression any crowd receives of you is a good one.

Run in with enthusiasm—jumping and tumbling, if you can—to get the crowd fired up and make them want to cheer. Unlike track, however, you are not racing anyone, so make your entrance organized. Tumblers first, jumpers next run toward the crowd (as illustrated), double stunts at the back and sides. You should know your position on the field, or floor, and head for it without running into anyone else.

If you're hesitant, or walk in with your hands on your hips, you won't generate spirit. At the same time, you shouldn't grab the spotlight. The best cheerleaders never look as if they are showing off, because they aren't.

## Formations

Ever stop to consider how often some squads are seen in the same formation? Perhaps it's that same old straight line. Try some different ones to add variety and interest. For instance, a diagonal, square, or circle, are three. Here are more formations that can be adjusted easily to the size of your squad.

# FORMATIONS

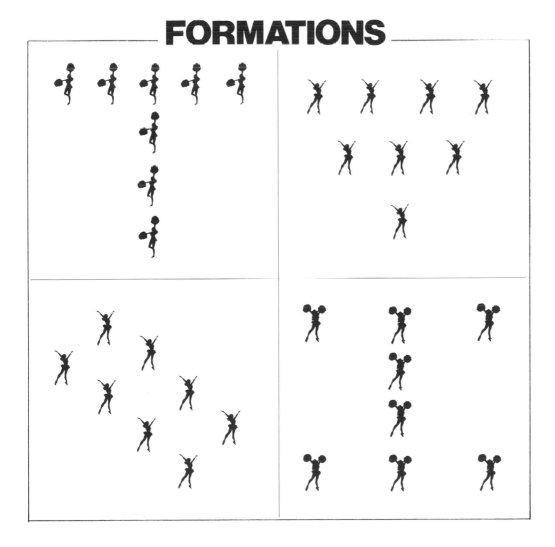

# FORMATIONS

# FORMATIONS

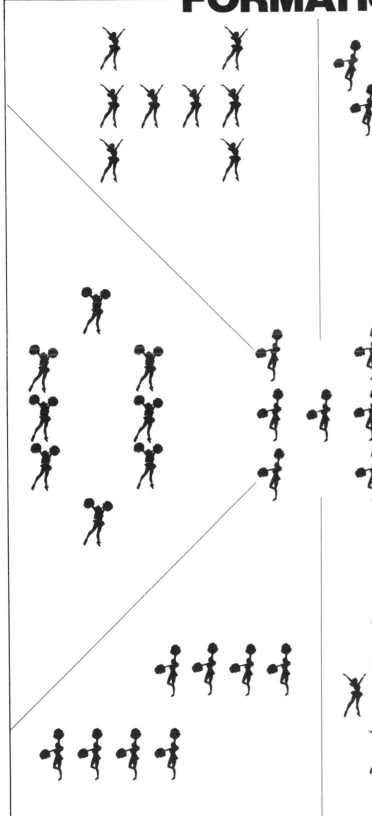

Always select a formation that does not interfere with the players' pregame warmup or with their strategy talk during time-out. Then, whatever you do, do it facing the crowd. A cheer loses its effectiveness when your back is turned because people can't see what you're doing or hear what you're saying. The NCA also recommends that taller squad members stand at the back of all formations.

In any formation, cheerleaders should line up from the front people. Therefore, it's essential that those up front be in the right spot. However, once you're on the field, there isn't much you, or anyone else, can do about it if they aren't. Certainly, you never want to yell at another squad member. If you've ever heard a spiritleader shout, "Bertha, move back, the line isn't straight," you know it sounds sloppy. The best you can do is be sure you're in your proper place and hope everyone else is too.

## Ready? Set!

To get a cheer started on the proper beat, a short, snappy signal should be used. But a top squad never uses a hand signal. Instead when a designated cheerleader (usually at the back of the formation) sees that all cheerleaders are set, he or she alerts squadmates and the crowd by saying "Ready-o, Let's go!" in a light, lively tone, or by using a short series of claps or counts. For variety, the same starting signal should not be used for all cheers. Make up some new signals of your own. Or take a look at this list of opening phrases:

> All Set? (Clap, clap.) You bet!
> Hey, ho. Let's go.
> Ready? Okay!
> Okay, take it away.
> All here? Let's cheer.
> Another cheer, let's hear.

## Perfect Timing

A cheer, like a song, should have rhythm. To really be effective, the rhythm of a cheer should have a steady beat—and every beat must have a motion. To be sure your cheers make the grade, the NCA has this advice:

- Don't cheer too fast, or your motions will run together. (Anyway, a crowd cannot cheer as fast as your squad.)

- Don't cheer too slow. Complicated gestures slow down the pace, so use simple motions that enable the cheer to flow smoothly.

- Don't have too many words for the motions, or vice versa.

- Don't have long pauses in your cheers. A pause should occur only when necessary to keep the beat.

## Incorporation

You should always incorporate jumps into a cheer as smoothly as possible. When incorporating double stunts and pyramids, the NCA suggests you remember these do's and don'ts.

- Keep yelling as you build. Never let there be silence.

- Don't break the rhythm of the cheer. If necessary, slow the entire cheer down so that you can build.

- Look at the crowd when mounting and dismounting, if possible.

- Always use proper spotting techniques in mounting and dismounting.

## Finishing Touches

All yells should end on a dynamic note rather than fade. An ending is as important as a beginning. For a dramatic ending, here are the options (which ones will work best for you is something your squad can decide):

- FREEZE means just that. Cheerleaders freeze in position for three full counts, then the crowd can tell the cheer is over.

- SPLITS look best when they are done in unison and saved for the end of a cheer, especially since it's often difficult for the cheerer to move out of the splits into another sequence.

- JUMPS. Squadmates should jump together as a squad, using the same type jump.

- Or choose a GYMNASTIC ENDING—a pyramid, double stunt, or tumbling. When you use a double stunt or pyramid ending, finish the cheer at the top with a big motion!

Don't use a double ending. It distracts from the cheer when everyone dismounts as a unit then slaps their thighs at the same time. Dismounts must be safe and organized. Cheerleaders who aren't spotting the dismount should attract the audience's attention by jumping.

## Impression Makers

There are a lot of dos and don'ts when you're a cheerleader that influence the opinion others form of you. So that the fans think only the best of you:

- Do watch the game.

- Don't run and talk to the other cheerleaders between cheers, or stand in a huddle talking about matters unrelated to the game.

- Do crouch down between cheers if there's a chance you may be interfering with spectators sitting behind you, trying to see the game.

- Do stand poised between cheers, not slouched.

- Don't laugh or make a face when you goof. A good cheerleader will continue the routine as if nothing happened, rather than losing his or her cool. Don't stand waiting for the squad to finish cheering, just keep going and keep smiling!

# Spreading the Word

Ho-hum chants are out; in are those that put spirit in the air because they're exhilarating and exciting.

It's a safe bet that at one time, all your school's cheers probably sounded great. But times do change and so do people. And you can't afford to stick with a cheer that's unrewarding. Not when you're shopping for a victory. Still, you shouldn't make the mistake of throwing out all your old cheers and starting completely over with all new. There are still plenty of people around who resist change. Take a good look at the shouts your squad uses and make sure they're something special.

## Choosing Your Words

No matter how catchy a yell is, or how snappily a squad presents it, a shout will not be effective if it's inappropriate or given at the wrong time. Top squads know better than to compete with the sports activity taking place. As a result, they save their cheering and chanting for between plays and during time-outs. Then they always select an eye-catching, *fitting* shout.

A cheer for the offense is appropriate when your school has the ball; cheer the defense when it's in the opponent's hands. Some cheers sound best when your team is winning, but they should be avoided when the rival is putting you down. Short shouts should be squeezed between plays or into time-outs. Between quarters, the longer ones are better.

Every squad should have a variety of cheers ready to motivate the team, whatever the situation. And along with that, the NCA recommends that your squad should

- Choose its cheers carefully.

- Take advantage of psychological moments when the crowd really feels like cheering.

- Never wear out a crowd by cheering or chanting too long, but do be sure to cheer enough.

## A Time to Cheer

There's a time to cheer, and a time not to cheer.

- Cheer when your team takes the floor or field.

- Cheer when a player for either team makes an exceptionally fine play.

- Cheer when a substitution is made on your team.

- Cheer in tribute to an injured player as he or she leaves the field.

- Cheer as encouragement.

- Cheer as much for the defense as the offense.

Whether you're winning or losing, an opponent being injured is nothing to cheer about. In fact, to do so is unforgivable. Same is true of cheering when an opposing band is playing. Banging the bleachers is out, too. The NCA cautions against cheering at any of these times:

- When signals are being called. (Teams appreciate quiet.)

- When an opposing player makes a mistake.

- When the rival team is penalized.

- When the game is in play.

- When rival spiritleaders, sharing a common side, are cheering.

- When an opposing player is taking a free throw.

No matter how much you're itching to yell, don't do it on

Quiet, please.

An opponent's injury is nothing to cheer about.

the field or court when officials are ready to resume play after a time-out, or near the coach and team when they're having a talk at the game.

## Do It Yourself

Let's face it. Hearing the same cheers month after month, year after year, can be boring. If there's a chance others are beginning to think your cheers are dull, put your free time to good use and strengthen your repertoire. All you have to do is pull out a paper and pencil and follow these five basic steps.

1.  Start with a good idea. For inspiration, consider current trends, slogans, and expressions. Keep in mind the sport for which you're cheering and the purpose for the cheer.
2.  Jot down a suitable, short, audience-appealing yell that has some action words in it. Remember, your cheer should have a rhythmic, steady beat, but not be singsong. Furthermore, a good yell isn't suggestive or a potential source of embarrassment to anyone. It shouldn't include references which are overly derogatory to an opponent.
3.  Experiment with the way the words sound. There are several effective ways of putting peppy sounds together.
4.  Combine the words with fresh motions and have fun while you do it. When a cheer is new, the gestures should be too. Keep in mind that every beat of the cheer should have a motion. If you put several words with just one cue, the crowd won't be able to follow you.

    For a lively look, vary the motions so the cheer won't drag. Change the gestures for each phrase. Doing so will give you a better opportunity to move about while yelling, and this enhances any cheer's looks.

    Always use large-scale motions, and make them as descriptive as possible without being silly. You already know that gestures should support the words of the cheer and add impact. (That's why you dream up the words first.) So if, for example, a cheer has the word *down,* be sure the matching gesture is in the appropriate direction. Also remember that action words need body movements. Words that imply force require the strongest, most vigorous gestures of all. Try such body actions as the lunge. Don't forget: Always end a yell on a dynamic note, then hold it to the count of three.
5.  Last, ask yourself these questions:

    •   Does the cheer fulfill the purpose for which it was planned?

- Are the words tailored to fit the purpose?

- Do the motions fit the words?

- Is the cheer snappy and easy to follow?

If you'd rather not create your own cheers, you can make up motions for the cheers that follow. Just keep the foregoing principles in mind.

The NCA happily shares its cheers for all seasons, for each and every reason. . . .

## Welcome Cheers

Whatever the season, send out a spirit of friendliness wherever you happen to be. Put a welcome cheer first on your list of shouts.

H–I  Hi!  We're glad to be here
H–I  Hi!  To give a welcome cheer!

He-e-e-y, We are here
To say hello
You've gotta give it a little body
And give it a little soul
You gotta give, Hey, Hey,
A big Hello!

The Tiger team is here
To do a Hello cheer
How have ya been?
We're glad to see ya again
The Tiger team says Hi!

Hello, Hello, Hello!
That's what we say to you
We wish you lots of luck
The whole game through
The Panthers say good luck
Ya know we do!

Hey, let's go
Let's give a big hello
We're here to say
Enjoy your stay
H-E-L-L-O!

## Opening Cheers

Out of tradition, some squads "fire up" their team by using the same opening shout game after game. Here are some yells you might want to consider.

### HEY, YOU OVER THERE
*(echo)*

Hey, you over there on the other side
We got a team that's backed by pride
We're gonna win without a doubt
We got that spirit, so shout it out!
Shout . . . Shout it out
Shout, shout, shout, shout it out
Shout . . . Shout it out
Shout, shout, shout, shout it out
You just SHOUT!

We got it—control!
There's no way stopping
That Lion's soul
We play to win
Come on, team (clap, clap), begin!

Here we come again
The Cats are trucking in
There's victory in the end
Wildcats—begin!

Things are hot and we can't be stopped
So let's move that red machine
Right up to the top—WE'RE HOT!

Panthers, dig in!
Go, fight, win
Let's begin
Go, fight, win
Panthers, dig in!

Watch out! We're here
So everybody stand clear
We're at the peak
Of our winning streak
So hey (clap)
Everybody stand clear!

Mighty Eagles, out to win
Mighty Eagles, let's begin
W-I-N (slap)
Let's win!

Hey, you've gotta cheer
To let 'em know we're here
So cheer (clap, clap)
We're here!

We're here
And ready to cheer
We're here
For another great year
We're here
So let's cheer!

## Short Game Cheers

When time's at a premium between football plays, or during a brief time-out, these are the cheers to do.

Take it to the top, hey!
Tigers gonna win it (clap)
Tiger team is running hot
Let's take it to the limit!

We've . . . got
What it takes
To make our team
Super-r-r GREAT!

Go for the victory
Go for the team
Fight for the Longhorns
We got steam!

Get power together—energize!
Make this team unified
Together—to fight
Hey, hey, all right!

Stop that team
Show 'em what we mean
Go, Bears (clap, clap, clap)
Go, Bears (clap, clap, clap)
Go, Bears!

We've got the power
We've got the might
We've got the spirit
To beat 'em tonight!

We can't be defeated
We must have success
The Eagle team is Number One
Yes, we are the best!

We've got spirit, hey!
S-P-I-R-I-T
S-P-I-R-I-T
Badger spirit never dies
Never, never, NEVER!

Hey, let's go
Hey, let's fight
Hey, fire up
Let's win tonight!

We're ready to go
We're ready to fight
F-I-G-H-T
(clap, clap) Victory!

## Game Cheers

Here are some longer words of encouragement for the team when there's an extended time-out. If you like, you can also use them at half time and rallies.

Fight, Raiders, fight (clap, clap)
It's time to win tonight (clap, clap)
We got the power
We got the might—
Let's win tonight!

Get up, get down!
Turn yourself around!
You're in the groove
Get on the move
Get up, get down!

Gotta get it together
Gotta fight (clap)
Come on, let's do it!
Gotta get it together
Gotta F-I-G-H-T
Fight!

We're on the move, so wind up!
No time to lose, so wind up!
We're gettin down
We're the best around
Come on, team,
Let's wind up!

Move on over, we're comin through
We're gonna show you what we can do
So move on over, we're comin through—
The Bulldog team is after you!

Game time for the Lancer team
Wind it up, (clap) hey!
Set the clock, now fans let's rock
Wind it up, (clap) hey!
Game time, let's take it to the top!

Fire up (clap, clap)
Fire up, up, up—
Fire up (clap, clap)
Fire up, up, up—
Sparks are flyin'
Cause we are tryin'
To fire up (clap, clap)
Fire up, up, up!

Up and down
Our team don't mess around
Cause—we are the best
From the east to the west
And when our team is up
You're down!

On the move, hey, hey
To win today
Go all the way, hey, hey
We'll win today
All right, all right, all right, Hey!

The Indians are hot (clap)
And can't be stopped
We'll take you 'round and 'round
We'll beat you up and down (clap)
The Indians are HOT!

Hustle, haven't you heard?
Hustle, yeah, that's the word!
The ultimate way to show your might
Is hustle, team, and fight, fight, fight!

We've done it—when? Before!
We'll do it—when? Again!
And you'll know when—we Win!

Fight, Falcons, fight!
Swift as a laser light
Falcons, the force
Is with you tonight!

We're gonna fight with all our might
We're gonna win this game tonight
We're gonna beat (clap, clap, clap, clap)
   Tigers (clap, clap, clap, clap)
Beat (clap, clap, clap, clap) Tigers (clap, clap,
   clap, clap)
(Clap, clap, clap, clap, clap) BEAT TIGERS!

Hey, clap your hands
(Stomp, clap, stomp, clap, clap
Stomp, clap, stomp, clap, clap)
Hey, all you Tigers fans
Stand up and clap your hands
(Repeat stomp claps)
Hey now, get in the beat
Stand up and move your feet
(Repeat stomp claps)
Hey now, get in the groove
This time let's really move
(Repeat stomp claps three times)
HEY, LET'S MOVE!

## Game Cheers—Offense

Offense, you can do it!
It's our ball so let's get to it!
Make that defense pay their toll
Push that ball across that goal!

Look, they've got what we've got
So we need more, hey!
Come on, big team,
Let's raise that score!

(Clap) OFFENSE, dig in!
O-F-F-E-N-S-E
Offense, dig in!

Ease on down that line
It's Tiger victory time
We've got that ball
We're doing fine
So ease on down that line!

S - S,  C - C,  O-R-E
Score, Bears,
We want a Victory!

Score six points
Take it down to that goal
S-I-X
Score six!

Hey, Mustangs are great
Hey, Mustangs just wait
We've got the ball
Don't hesitate
Mustangs are great!

Sink that ball
On through that rim,
Go for two
Mighty Lions, let's win!

## Game Cheers—Defense

Block the Mounties
Don't let them through
Block the Mounties
We depend on you!

Hold that line
Defense—you can do it
Don't waste time
Defense—let's get to it
Hold that line!

Defense, defense,
Show your might
Stop 'em, hold 'em
Fight, team, fight!

Roll 'em over and power 'em down
We've got the mightiest defense
Around!

Hey, red! Hey, black!
Attack and sack that quarterback
It's up to you, break through!

Hey, hey, hey
Let's take that ball away
Hey, hey, take it away
(Slap, clap) OKAY!

Tighten up that line
Don't let 'em through
Defense, defense,
We depend on you!

Come on, big D, hold tight
Let's win this game tonight
We got the power
We got the might
Come on, defense, hold tight!

## Mascot Cheers

Bears are lookin' good (clap, clap, clap)
Bears are lookin' fine (clap, clap, clap)
Bears are outta sight
Bears are DYN-O-MITE!

Longhorns—you're tough
Longhorns—you're tough
Those Cats are turning back
They must have met their match
Hey! Longhorns—you're tough!

Tigers comin'—they're on their way
Tigers chargin'—they're here to stay
Tigers—say hey!

All right, okay
Mighty Lions are here to stay
All right, okay
Mighty Lions all the way
All right, OKAY!

The Raiders are great, the best in the state
The Raiders are neat, they can't be beat
The Raiders are rough, the Raiders are tough
They'll make you spin, GO, FIGHT, WIN!

Vikings are here to show you where it's at
Vikings gonna getcha
Vikings gonna getcha
Vikings gonna getcha
If you don't watch out!

Hornets, Hornets, hear our call
Hornets, Hornets, get that ball
Hornets, Hornets, raise that score
Hornets, Hornets, WE WANT MORE!

Tigers, Tigers, that's our name
Tigers, Tigers, let's win this game
T-I-G-E-R-S
Tigers, Tigers, YES, YES, YES!

## Color Cheers

The brightest, the best—these are the cheers you wouldn't want to be without!

Hey, what about (snap, snap)
A color shout (snap, snap)
RED, RED, RED, RED
BLUE, BLUE, BLUE, BLUE
Hey, what about (snap, snap)
A color shout (snap, snap)
RED, RED, RED, RED
BLUE, BLUE, BLUE, BLUE
Hey, what about (snap, snap)
A SHOUT!

Red—Blue
Blue—Blue
Mighty Knights are after you
Go, go
Fight, fight
MIghty Knights (stomp, clap),
All right!

GREEN—WHITE
Get in gear!
GREEN—WHITE
Victory near
SHAMROCKS
IN THE CLEAR!

Hold 'em, hold 'em
Fight, fight, fight
Don't let 'em score
On the Blue and White!

Red Red Red, White White White
University High School
Fight, fight, fight
(This cheer may be varied by placing claps in
    between the colors)

## Victory Cheers

Rise up to victory
And conquer the Bears (clap, clap)
Celebrate cause we are great
And conquer (slap) the Bears!

Victory's the word
In the Lion crowd
Victory is heard
Shout it out loud
What's the word? VICTORY
What is heard? VICTORY
Victory, Lions, VICTORY!

Take a V (clap, clap, clap)
Add an I (clap, clap, clap)
Try a C (clap, clap, clap)
T-O-R-Y (clap, clap, clap)
V-I-C-T-O-R-Y
Victory, victory
It's victory tonight!

V—I-C—T-O-R-Y
We spell out our battle cry
Trojans are here
To win tonight
Come on, team,
Show 'em your might!

## Crowd Participation Cheers and Chants

Shout, shout (clap) out loud,
Shout, shout (clap) we're proud,

We'll shout (clap) loud 'cause we are proud,
Shout, shout (clap) out loud!
Shout, shout (clap) we'll win,
Shout, shout (clap) again
We'll shout to win, we'll do it again,
Shout, shout (clap), let's win!

| (Cheerleaders) | (Crowd) |
|---|---|
| WE GOT RAZ-MA-TAZ | RAZ-MA-TAZ |
| Like no one else has, | RAZ-MA-TAZ |
| We got a real fine coach | RAZ-MA-TAZ |
| We think that he's the most, | RAZ-MA-TAZ |
| We got a real super starting five, | RAZ-MA-TAZ |
| They'll eat you up alive, | RAZ-MA-TAZ |
| We've got a talented band, | RAZ-MA-TAZ |
| Let's give 'em a hand, | RAZ-MA-TAZ |
| We got a great mascot, | RAZ-MA-TAZ |
| We think that he is tops, | RAZ-MA-TAZ |
| We got S-S, P-P, I-I, R-R, I-I, T-T, | |
| SPIRIT, SPIRIT, SPIRIT! | |

I've got a feeling in my soul
(Repeat)
And I just gotta get it out
(Repeat)
It's boogie fever and it's outa control
(Repeat)
So boogie to the beat and shout!
(Repeat)
Boogie fever, boogie fever, boogie fever
Boogie to the beat and shout! (clap, clap, clap)
Boogie fever, boogie fever, boogie fever
Boogie to the beat and shout! (clap, clap, clap)

Get it, got it, good—got it?
No-o-o-o-o-o-o-o-o
Get it, got it, good—got it?
No-o-o-o-o-o-o-o-o
Get it, got it, good—got it?
No-o-o-o-o-o-o-o-o
You gotta get, get, get, get, get it,
And when you got it—you're good!
(Repeat three times)
Get it? Got it! Good!

We're fired up and ready
We're fired up and ready
Our team is alive
Our team is alive
We're fired up and ready
We're fired up and ready
I wouldn't tell you no lie
I wouldn't tell you no lie
So let's go—GO
So let's fight—FIGHT
We got the power to beat 'em tonight!
(Repeat)

Lion team is really hot
Lion team is really hot
We got something that you ain't got
We got something that you ain't got
We got the soul now, we got the beat
We got the soul now, we got the beat
To set those Wildcats on their seat
To set those Wildcats on their seat!
(Repeat)

| (Cheerleaders) | (Crowd) |
|---|---|
| Hey, crowd | Yeah, baby |
| Ya got spirit? | Well, maybe |
| Hey, crowd | Yeah, baby |
| Ya got the team? | Well, maybe |
| Hey, crowd | Yeah, baby |
| Ya gonna win it? | Well, maybe |
| What us got? | Us got a lot |
| Us got a team that's red-hot! | |

## Divided or Competitive Cheers

| | |
|---|---|
| *Cheerleaders:* | Sophomores, are you with us? |
| *Sophomores:* | Yeaaaaaaa man. |
| *Cheerleaders:* | Juniors, are you with us? |
| *Juniors:* | Yeaaaaaaa man. |
| *Cheerleaders:* | Seniors, are you with us? |
| *Seniors:* | Yeaaaaaaa man. |
| *Cheerleaders:* | Well, let's give fifteen for that wonderful team. |

(Fifteen rahs)

| | |
|---|---|
| *First section:* | HEY! HEY! |
| *Second section:* | What 'ya say? |
| *First section:* | HEY! HEY! |
| *Second section:* | What 'ya say? |
| *Everyone:* | LOOKS LIKE BULLDOGS ALL THE WAY! |

| | |
|---|---|
| *Sophomores:* | V-I-C-T-O-R-Y that's the Sophomore battle cry |
| *Juniors:* | V-I-C-T-O-R-Y that's the Junior battle cry |
| *Seniors:* | V-I-C-T-O-R-Y that's the Senior battle cry |
| *Everyone:* | V-I-C-T-O-R-Y VICTORY! |

## Football Chants

Determination makes us move
The Hoover Hawks are in the groove!

In the air and on the ground
Marshall Bears don't mess around!

They haven't scored yet,
Hurry up and intercept!

Hustle down for six
Cats, show them all your tricks!

Hey crowd, stand up and yell
Grab that B-A double L!

Hey, don't take no jive
Get that ball and come alive!

Wind it up and let it go
We got to score, come on let's go!

Hang on—we're coming on strong
Hang on—it won't be long
Hang on—for victory
Raider team is history!

Touchdown, touchdown
Do it again!
Touchdown, touchdown
To win!

A-T-T, A-C-K, ATTACK
The quarterback
Push him back!

Defense, defense, hold that line!
Defense, defense, hold that line!

Take that ball around the left end,
Take that ball around the right,
Take that ball straight up the middle,
And fight tonight!

Offense keep going!
We gotta roll, you're all we got so
Offense keep going!
Offense keep going!
We gotta roll, you're all we got so
Offense keep going!

Intercept that pass and
Run real fast!
Intercept that pass and
Run real fast!

Defense, hold that line, hey!
Defense, hold that line, hey!

## Basketball Chants

Get on down, get on down, get on down that floor (clap)
Get on down, get on down, down that floor and score!

Down that floor, hey, hey
Down that floor, hey, hey
Two more, hey, hey
Two more!

Hey, let's go
Make that free throw!
Hey, let's go
Make that free throw!

Tip it (clap), tip it (clap), tip it to a Bulldog, hey, hey!
Tip it (clap), tip it (clap), tip it to a Bulldog, hey, hey!
Tip it (clap), tip it (clap), tip it to a Bulldog!

Fever, we're really hot,
Fever, gonna make that shot,
Set you up, just to let you down,
Look out, Lions, we've come to town!

Settle down, settle down
Get that ball and go!
(Repeat)

Brian, Brian, jump real high
Hit the ball to a Tiger guy!
(Repeat)

Tiger team, we sure are hot,
Tiger team, let's shoot that shot!

See that basket
See that rim
Come on, Comets,
Put it in!

When it rains (clap) it pours (clap)
Colts gonna score!
When it rains (clap) it pours (clap)
Colts gonna score!

Shoot it high, shoot it low
In the net the ball must go!
Shoot it high, shoot it low
In the net the ball must go!

GO! GO!
Where? Where?
We want a basket
Over there!
(Everyone stands and points to the basket on "Over
    there")

Pass that ball,
Drop it in,
Central High School
WIN WIN WIN!

Dribble, dribble down the floor
Shoot the ball and raise that score!
Raise that score!

Hey hey what do you say?
Let's take the ball away!

Tip it, tip it,
Tip it to a Bulldog!

How about a basket?
How about a score?
We've got some
But we want more.

Catch it—pass it
Dribble down the floor
Shoot that basket
Score, score, SCORE!

Come on, Central, burn that floor,
Come on, Central, raise that score,
You can win, don't give in,
Come on, Central, let's begin!

S-I-N-K
Sink it, Sam, sink it!

Dribble it (stomp stomp)
Pass it (stomp stomp)
Dribble it, pass it
We want a basket

Sink it through
We want two
Sink it for two!

Shoot it, pass it
Dribble down the floor
We want a basket
Score score SCORE!

Zip zip zippy,
Zap zap zappy,
H-A-P-P-Y we're happy!

You wanna take away my gusto?
You wanna take away my pride?
Well, you can't take my gusto
And you can't have my pride
'Cause the mighty Knights are movin'
And leaving you behind!

We are the Raiders (clap), we got the beat (clap, clap)
So get down and move your feet,
Say (stomp, clap, stomp, stomp, clap, stomp)
Raiders Raiders Raiders!
(stomp, clap, stomp, stomp, clap, stomp)
Do it, do it, do it!

G—O-O-O-O-O—go go!
G—O-O-O-O-O—go go!
G—O-O-O-O-O—go go!

Go big team hey!
Go big team hey!

We got you now, we can't be beat,
The Tiger team is really neat,
We got you now, we can't be stopped,
The Tiger team is on the top!

Score score,
Score score,
Eagles, let's
Get some more!

Hey Tigers, win this game,
Give those Bears some more of the same!

We got spirit, yes we do
We got spirit, how about you!
(Repeat)

B-I-N-G-O  Bingo!
B-I-N-G-O  Bingo!
One for the money
Two for the show
We got ya beat
BINGO!

R . . . A . . . L-L-Y
Let's rally, yeah let's rally
(clap clap clap)
(Repeat)

Get up—NCA's here
Get on up, get up
Get up and cheer
Get on up, get up, NCA's here to cheer
Get on up, get on up, get on up!

I said      V  (stomp, stomp, clap)
            I  (stomp, stomp, clap)
            C  (stomp, stomp, clap)
            T-O-R-Y!
(Repeat)

Knock knock
Who's there?
The Tiger team and you'd better beware!
(Repeat)

P-P-P-P-P-P-P-POWER,  POWER
P-P-P-P-P-P-P-POWER,  POWER
P-P-P-P-P-P-P-POWER,  POWER!

We got the Bear beat
We got the Bear beat
(Stomp, clap, stomp, clap, stomp, clap)
Beat 'em, Bears!
(Repeat)

Hey, you're crazy
You think you're real cool
You thought that we were lazy
But you ran out of fuel
Hey, you're losin'
You found out we've got class
We must have been confusin'
'Cause you ran out of gas!

Romp 'em, stomp 'em
Knock them down, hey, hey!
(Repeat)

Big G, little O, go, go
Big G, little O, go, go!
(Repeat)

S-O-U-L
With a little bit of soul
You can do so well!
(Repeat)

Fe, fi, fo, fum
We got soul, now you get some!
(Repeat)

We got the fever, we're hot
We can't be stopped!
(Repeat)

Hey, hey, what do ya say
Tigers, Tigers all the way!
(Repeat)

S-O-U-L
Soul team, sock it to 'em now!
(Repeat)

We got the super soul spirit
We got the SSS!
(Repeat)

Go, go, get 'em, get 'em
ooh, ah!
(Repeat)

Go, go, Vikings!
Fight tonight,
Go, go, Vikings!
Fight tonight!

Hey, hey, hey, hey, hey,
Take it away!
Hey, hey, hey, hey, hey,
Take it away!

Look up (clap), be bold (clap)
Spartan spirit, take a hold (clap)
Look up (clap), be bold (clap)
Spartan spirit, take a hold! (clap)

You gotta get down (clap, clap)
You gotta get down and fight!
You gotta get down (clap, clap)
You gotta get down and fight!

Break away, Tigers, get down that line,
Break away, Tigers, it's scoring time,
Say move it (clap), break away,
Say groove it (clap), break away,
Say, Tigers (clap), movin' your way!

## Rhythm Chants

Fresh (clap) and hot (clap)
We'll show you what we got! (clap)
(Repeat)
N (clap) C A (clap)
Will boogie down today (clap)
(Repeat)
Clap (clap) your hands (clap)
Get on your feet and jam (clap)
(Repeat)
Show what you got (clap)
Everybody, do the robot (clap)
(Repeat)
Move (clap) your bustle (clap)
Come on and hustle (clap)
(Repeat)
Release (clap) your anguish (clap)
Everybody, let's body language (clap)
(Repeat)
This ain't (clap) no prank (clap)
Come on and spank (clap)
(Repeat)
I learned (clap) to skirm (clap)
And now (clap) the worm (clap)
(Repeat)
I said fresh (clap) and hot (clap)
We'll show you what we got! (clap)

Wind it up!
Can you boogie? Yeah
Can you boogie? Yeah
Wind it up (clap), wind it up (clap)
I'm your boogie-woogie baby,
If you want to see me boogie,
All you gotta do is wind me up, hey!
Wind it up (clap), wind it up (clap)
Can you boogie? Yeah
Can you boogie? Yeah
Wind it up (clap), wind it up (clap)
I'm your boogie-woogie baby,
If you want to see me boogie,
All you gotta do is wind me up, hey!

Take your time and move it down that line
We're off to score so let's give one big roar
S—C—U-R-E let's score (clap, clap), let's score (clap,
　　clap)
S—C—O-R-E let's score (clap, clap), let's score (clap,
　　clap)
S—C—O-R-E let's score (clap, clap), let's score!

The disco scene has come alive
And for the Tiger team that ain't no jive,
We got the muscle to do the hustle!
We're on top, the bus stop!
We got the pep to five step!
(Repeat)

Slip slidin' away!
(Repeat)
You're gonna slip!
(Repeat)
You're gonna slide!
(Repeat)
Slip, slip, slide, slide,
Eagles got pride!

Superman lives in a telephone booth
After this game you gonna know the truth
Hey, hey, go, go, go, hey, hey, go, go, go
Kiss your mama, kiss your pappy
Winnin' this game gonna make us happy
Hey, hey, go, go, go, hey, hey, go, go, go
When you squeeze lemons, you get juice
When you play us, it ain't no use
Hey, hey, go, go, go, hey, hey, go, go, go
Shake your left foot, shake your right
Because our team is dyn-o-mite
Hey, hey, go, go, go, hey, hey, go, go, go
Rollercoaster, do that roll, rollercoaster
Right to that goal
Hey, hey, go, go, go, hey, hey, go, go, go!

That boogie beat
Hey, that boogie beat
Everytime I hear that beat, I want to shout HEY!
It goes na na na, na na na na na na—na
(Repeat)
Ahhh that boogie beat
Hey, that boogie beat
Ahh that's just one beat I could not do without, HEY!
It goes na na na, na na na na na na—na
(Repeat)

We're not (clap, clap) gonna take it
We're not (clap, clap) gonna take it
Tiger's think they're really cool
(Repeat chorus once)
Panthers comin' down on you
(Repeat chorus once)
So get that feelin' in your soul
(Repeat chorus once)
And let 'em know who's in control
(Repeat chorus once)
Are you (clap, clap) gonna take it?
We're not (clap, clap) gonna take it
We're not, we're not, we're not
Gonna take it!

There's a new kind of beat going round, getting down,
There's a whole lot of rhythm going round
Oh, we've got the beat (clap, clap)
That Tiger beat
Oh, we've got the beat (clap, clap)
That Tiger beat!

Shake and boogie (clap)
It's easy to do (clap)
Shake and boogie (clap)
It's something brand-new (clap)
Shake, shake, shake! Shake, shake, shake!
Shake and boogie! Shake and boogie!
(Repeat)

Go, let's do it
Let's go for the Tiger team
Here we go now
G-G-O let's go for the Tiger team (clap, clap)
Fight, let's do it
Let's fight for the Tiger team
Here we go now
F-I-G-H-T—let's fight for the Tiger team (clap, clap)
Win, let's do it
Let's win for the Tiger team
Here we go now
W-I-N—let's win for the Tiger team!

We got it, we got it, we got it, hey, hey
You want it, you want it, you want it, hey, hey
It's in my head, that's what I said
It's in my eye, oh my
It's in my nose, there it goes
It's In my mouth, makes me shout
It's in my chin, we're gonna win
It's in my shoulder, makes me bolder
It's in my chest, we're the best
It's in my thigh, oh my
It's in my feet, we can't be beat
It's in the ground, it's all around
It's in the air, it's everywhere
It's on the moon, it's coming soon
It's on the sun, we're number one
We got it, we got it, we got it, hey, hey
You want it, you want it, you want it, hey, hey
What is it?
THE GOOD OLE BEARCAT SPIRIT!

Aw shucks, you're too much
You're out of sight, you're all right
But can you dig it?
Yeah, we can dig it
We can dig it to the left
We can dig it to death
But can you dig it?
Yeah, we can dig it
We can dig it to the right
We can dig it all night
But can you dig it?
Yeah, we can dig it
We can dig it on the floor
We can dig it out the door
But can you dig it?
Yeah, we can dig it
We can dig it on the ceiling
We can dig it with feeling
But can you dig it?
Yeah, we can dig it
We can dig it in the stands
We can dig it with our fans
But can you dig it?
Yeah, we can dig it
We can dig it with our toes
'Cause the feeling grows and grows
But can you dig it?
Yeah, we can dig it
We can dig it with our feet
'Cause the TIGERS CAN'T BE BEAT!

You say your team is up,
I say your team is down
'Cause it just so happens,
That we're the best around!
So just accept it, don't reject it,
You can't defy it, so don't deny it!
We're number one, we're number one (clap, clap)
We're number one, we're number one (clap, clap)
Raiders to the left, Raiders to the right
You're stuck here in the middle,
No wonder you're uptight!
So just accept it, don't reject it,
You can't defy it, so don't deny it!
We're number one, we're number one! (clap, clap)
We're number one, we're number one! (clap, clap)
We're number one, we're number one!


Hey, you Vikings—hey, you Vikings,
Somebody's calling your name
Somebody's calling your name
Hey, you Vikings—hey, you Vikings,
Somebody's playing your game
Somebody's playing your game
Tic toc—can't stop the Vikings
Can't stop, can't stop the Vikings!
(Repeat)


Red lights are flashing
You better get back
'Cause the Mustang locomotive
Is rolling down the track
Choo-choo-choo-choo-choo-choo
Red lights are flashing
You better let us through
Or the Mustang locomotive
Will roll right over you!
Choo-choo-choo-choo-choo-choo!!
(Repeat faster each time)

We got the team that's doin' us right! (Repeat)
We got the players fired up tonight! (Repeat)
We got the team that sure is fine! (Repeat)
We got the players that'll blow your mind! (Repeat)
We got the team that's gonna win! (Repeat)
We got the players, let's do it again! (Repeat)

Take it to the limit
Take it to the limit
Take it to the max
Take it to the max
We're the mighty Warriors (clap)
We're the mighty Warriors (clap)
Show you where it's at (clap)
Show you where it's at (clap)
Boom sha boom, sha boom boom boom (clap, clap)
Boom sha boom, sha boom boom boom (clap, clap)
Boom sha boom, sha boom boom boom! (clap, clap)

You may be big, it may be true,
But we're gonna walk all over you!
Hey, hey (clap), it's over,
Cry on (clap) my shoulder!
You may be rough, you may be tough,
But we're gonna show you all our stuff!
Hey, hey (clap), it's over,
Cry on (clap) my shoulder!
You may be mean, you may be bad,
I tell you people you've just been had!
Hey, hey (clap), it's over,
Cry on (clap) my shoulder!
Sob, sob, boo hoo!
Look out, Lions, we're gonna get you!

Losin's not our game,
'Cause it won't bring you fame!
To make the headlines you see,
You've got to win consistently!
We came to play (clap), Hey!
We came to play! (clap)

We read it in the papers, just the other day
We read the mighty Tigers are really on their way
They have done it before and they can do it again
Hey, the mighty, mighty Tigers are gonna win again!

I'd like to make one thing perfectly clear
Your team's as unstable as the national prices
You can't put an end to the energy crisis
You're behind the times and out of date
You've probably been involved in Watergate
You're bad news (snap, snap, snap)
You're gonna lose (snap, snap, snap)
You're bad news (snap, snap, snap)
You're gonna lose!

Ring—a ding—ding, ding dong, ding a-dong
Ring—a ding—ding, ding dong, ding a-dong
Dial long distance, Operator 2
But you won't get our number, 'cause we're listed
    in *Who's Who*
(Repeat chorus)
Try calling us, you'll waste your dime
'Cause we are the Lions and we'll ring your chimes
(Repeat chorus)
Dial our number, you won't get through
But heed the recording, don't call us 'cause we'll
    call you
(Repeat chorus)
We accept collect, but not from you
'Cause we are No. 1 and you're only No. 2
(Repeat chorus)—Click!

T-C-B, T-C-B
We're taking care of business
Let us demonstrate, hey
We're taking care of business
We infuriate
T-C-B, T-C-B
We're taking care of business
Now watch us pursue
We're taking care of business
And our business is you!

# Camping Out

Now that you're a cheerleader, when you think of summer, think about putting your schoolbooks away, basking in the sun, and loading up a van or two to spend a week at an NCA clinic.* It's the perfect place for any squad to reach its highest potential.

At camp your squad can pick up new ideas for cheers, chants, skits, and pompon routines that are guaranteed to add excitement to your rallies. While learning to work together as a group, you'll also acquire new skills in gym-

At camp you'll learn to work together as a squad.

* Write the NCA for dates and locations of the more than three hundred Superstar Spirit Camps held each year.

nastics, tumbling, mini-tramp, partner stunts, and pyramid building. What's more, you'll learn all of these things from the most talented and experienced instructors in the country.

Every evening there's a workshop on goal setting and interpersonal relationships, and there's an evaluation session. For these, cheerleaders need to bring four of their own cheers. Each night, they will be asked to perform one of their own cheers plus one they have learned at camp. An evaluation group will help everyone improve his or her technique regardless of personal style.

## What to Bring

Wherever and however you go, be sure to plan ahead. Since most NCA clinics are held outdoors, you can't beat the comfort of shorts and T-shirts. Cotton ones are great because cotton is the coolest fabric you can put next to your skin.

Bring everything you need.

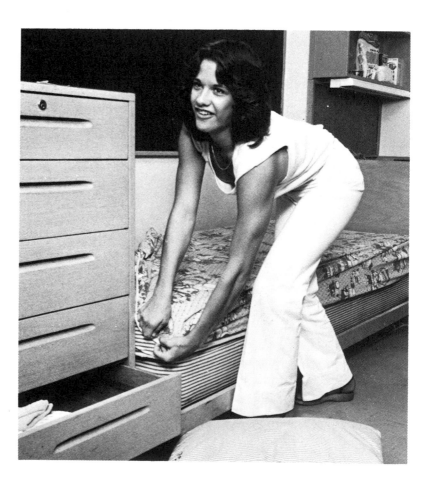

Many squads get set for camp by buying or making matching outfits so they can be identified as a squad. These outfits can be any color you'd like and certainly don't have to be expensive. The only definite *outs* in camp clothes are bare tops of any kind. When you're tumbling and building pyramids, these tops just aren't a good choice. Besides, you'll need protection from the sun.

Tennis shoes are a must, so make sure yours are comfortable. Foot specialists advise against buying any shoes you have to break in; they should be comfortable when you buy them.

Since most NCA camps are held on college campuses, you are asked to bring your own linens. Pack sheets, a pillow, pillowcase, blanket, towels, and washcloths. You'll need your personal health care needs. If you like, bring a camera, Thermos, pompons, alarm, postage for letters, spending money, notebook, stationery, and pen. Don't bring any jewelry, but do bring a uniform to wear for a squad photograph if the Idea sounds appealing. And don't forget a sweater or jacket. A typical day runs from seven in the morning to nine at night, with little time to spare. At some camps there are swimming facilities, but most cheerleaders use any free time to rest, practice, or jot off a quick note to a friend at home.

While at camp, you are not allowed to date or have overnight guests or off campus visitors. So before you leave home, be sure friends and relatives understand this.

# Doin' Fine

Practice makes perfect. You've been hearing that for years. It happens to be true. The only way to be the best you can possibly be is to work at being good. What's more, when you're a cheerleader, it's unfair to all the other squad members if you aren't.

## Practice, Practice, Practice

If you're the squadmate who can't seem to get it right no matter how hard you try, simply spend extra time on those routines that are difficult for you. Be assured, you're bound to succeed if you keep trying.

At the same time, if you happen to learn faster than the rest of the group, devote your time to assisting those who are in need of extra help. It shows when a group works together. And your squad wants to display a synchronized, precisionlike look. It takes cooperation and hours and hours of practice to develop this look. Ideally, you should practice every weekday except the day of the game.

Whether or not your practice sessions are supervised by the coach, it's up to you to attend them faithfully and spend your time wisely by building on what you have mastered. This doesn't mean you still can't have fun. Just make every minute count with these ten tips from the NCA:

1. Arrive on time, ready for practice, and set to GO for ninety minutes. (At the NCA, being on time means arriving five minutes before you're expected.)

2. Always start with warmups to strengthen and stretch those muscles.

3. Then practice jumps. First, work on form and height. Next, try coordinating them as a squad.

4. Practice cheers and chants for the upcoming game. Note those that still need work.

5. Take a ten-minute break, then get right back to business.

6. Practice new yells, motions, formations and pompon routines, giving special attention to those you want for the next game.

7. Take time to observe the cheers and check for techniques, timing, spacing, and an upbeat sound. (Some schools improve their practice sessions by videotaping them.)

8. Work on trouble spots. Then work some more, until the group feels comfortable and confident doing the cheer.

9. Talk about upcoming projects, send-off rallies, and problems.

10. Agree on a time to work on pep rallies, skits, and posters.

## Squad Unity

One of the secrets of a successful squad is unity. This strength comes when *all* members are equally committed to common goals. But even then, the unity doesn't just happen automatically. It requires a special effort on the part of each teammate. As the NCA points out, it takes an entire squad to build unity; however, one member less dedicated, determined, or devoted can make it fail.

Trouble generally starts when hard feelings exist within a group. If there are hidden resentments, intersquad communications are usually strained. And when the lines of communication are down, nobody benefits.

When there's a disagreement or misunderstanding, you should be mature enough to deal constructively with the problem. It's always best to talk things over rationally and calmly within the group. Going outside the squad with criticism is counterproductive. Hiding your annoyance from the squad is unhealthy, too. And certainly, storming off doesn't help at all! It does help to remember that no one can be right all the time.

A squad doesn't have to agree on everything. But it's important that you all share major objectives. Mutual aims that all squadmates are willing to work toward increase the effectiveness of the group.

There's no better time for a squad to set realistic expectations than soon after you've been elected. As a group, cheerleaders should outline their plans. The process through which the goals are achieved is often as important as the goals themselves.

When making your list, refer to the obligations of a spiritleader on pages 3-5.

Every cheerleading squad should have a *constitution*, or set of by-laws, which is the governing force of the squad. This constitution should reflect the school's philosophy as well as the goals established within the squad.

With a sponsor's guidance, cheerleaders should set forth rules and regulations they believe will increase the effectiveness of the group. Then these guidelines should be enforced by your advisor.

A copy of the school's cheerleading constitution should be included in the tryout pack or posted before tryouts begin. Then those who have expressed an interest in becoming a spiritleader will know before they are selected what rules must be abided by and what disciplinary action will be taken should a rule be broken.

Here's an NCA checklist of what a constitution should include

- Conduct and responsibilities (code of ethics)

- Uniforms and appearance (when worn, care, hair, jewelry, makeup, equipment, financial responsibilities)

- Game attendance

- Practice sessions (policy regarding missing practice and summer camp; excused and unexcused absences)

- Academic requirements

- Transportation

- Suspension and dismissal (grounds for)

- Optional:

  Awards and banquets
  Resignation
  Tryouts—eligibility requirements, skills and procedure, judges, judging, and point system
  Conflict with other activities
  Responsibilities of the head cheerleader

See appendix for sample constitution.

# Knowing the Rules of the Game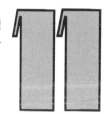

## Ground Rules

Only by understanding what is happening on the field or court can a cheerleader react appropriately and choose cheers wisely. Therefore, here are the basic rules of football and basketball every cheerleader should know. However, rules can and do change every year. So consult an athletic department at the beginning of the school year regarding any new rulings.

## Football

PLAYING SURFACE:   A level field.

PLAYING TIME:   A high school football game is forty-eight minutes long, divided into four twelve-minute *quarters. Half time* is a fifteen-to-twenty-minute rest period between the second and third quarters. In addition, there are two-minute intervals between quarters, during which the teams change goals.

THE CLOCK:   The clock is the official timer. It is stopped (1) after an incomplete pass; (2) after a team scores; (3) when a player is injured; (4) when the ball carrier goes out of bounds; and (5) when an official signals time-out. Each team receives four time-outs during each half.

TEAMS:   There are eleven players on each team.

PLAY: A kickoff starts the game. The kicking team is decided by a toss of a coin. The captain of the team winning the toss has his choice of kicking or receiving and can choose the goal his team will defend. The kicker place-kicks the ball from his team's forty-yard line.

A ball carrier is downed when any part of his body (other than his feet) and one hand touches the ground, or he goes out of bounds. Once the receiver of the kickoff has been downed, his team has four consecutive chances (*plays* or *downs*) to score or advance the ball a minimum of ten yards in order to keep possession of the football. If a team gains at least ten yards in four plays, the team has a *first down.* After each first down, the team with the ball gets another four downs to gain ten additional yards.

The team with the ball is called the *offensive team.* The other team is the *defensive team.*

The offensive team tries to advance the ball by running with it, passing it to another player, or kicking it. The defensive team tries to stop the offense from making forward progress.

Prior to each play, players meet in a team huddle. There, in a tight circle, they discuss the strategy that will enable them to outmaneuver their opponents. The two teams then line up facing each other along the *line of scrimmage,* an imaginary line defined by the ball's position that runs parallel to the yard lines.

Most plays start with the *quarterback* (standing directly behind the *center*) calling a series of numbers. These numbers are signals that indicate which play will be used and when it will begin. Although this decision has been made in the huddle, it is sometimes necessary to change a play at the line of scrimmage. A good quarterback can *read* defenses— or *keys* to what the defense is expecting the offense to do. Seeing the linebacker inch to the left, for example, means the defense is expecting a pass. Then the quarterback may change the play and call for a run. To do so, he uses an *audible*—a code word to announce to his teammates a new play is coming. Then he shouts the signals for the new play.

On the indicated count, the center snaps the ball through his legs to the quarterback. The quarterback can give the ball to one of the other *backs,* elect to keep it and run, or pass it to an *end.*

The offensive team loses possession of the ball if the ball carrier *fumbles* or drops the ball and a defensive player recovers it, if a defensive player intercepts a pass, or if the team fails to move ten yards in four tries.

A player in the backfield can kick (*punt*) the ball at any time. But a team rarely punts except on the fourth down, after it has failed to advance the ball ten yards, because the other team gains possession when they catch the ball. To punt, the kicker holds the ball in his hands, drops it, and kicks it before it touches the ground. The purpose of the punt is to move one's opponents as far from the goal lines as possible.

SCORING:   There are four ways to score in football. The first is a *touchdown* (which counts six points). It is scored by an offensive player carrying the ball over the goal line or by an offensive player catching a pass in the end zone. (A touch-down is scored when any part of the ball is on, above, or behind the goal line.)

After scoring a touchdown, a team tries for a *conversion*, an extra point after a touchdown. The team can score one point by kicking the ball over the crossbar between the goal-posts, or two points by running or passing the ball into the end zone, from the three-yard line—the point where it is put into play.

A *field goal*, which counts three points, is made by kicking the ball over the crossbar between the goalposts from any-where on the field. If missed, the ball is returned to the line of scrimmage, from which it was kicked, or twenty-yard line, whichever is farther from the goal line. A *safety*, worth two points, is scored by the defensive team when it downs the ball carrier in his own end zone, or if the ball carrier steps back out of his end zone.

OFFICIALS:   The *referee* is the chief official, and has overall control of the game. He stands behind the offensive team and blows a whistle to declare the ball *in play* (live) or *out of play* (dead). The *umpire* stands behind the defensive line and watches for fouls in the line. The *head linesman* stands at one end of the line of scrimmage and marks the forward progress of the ball. He also supervises the *marking crew*, which moves up and down one sideline keeping track of the downs and the distance gained. Cheerleaders take their cues from the men holding this job when an electronic scoreboard or announcer isn't alerting them as to yardage gained on a given play. The *field judge* stands on the opposite side of the field from the head linesman and is responsible for officially timing the game.

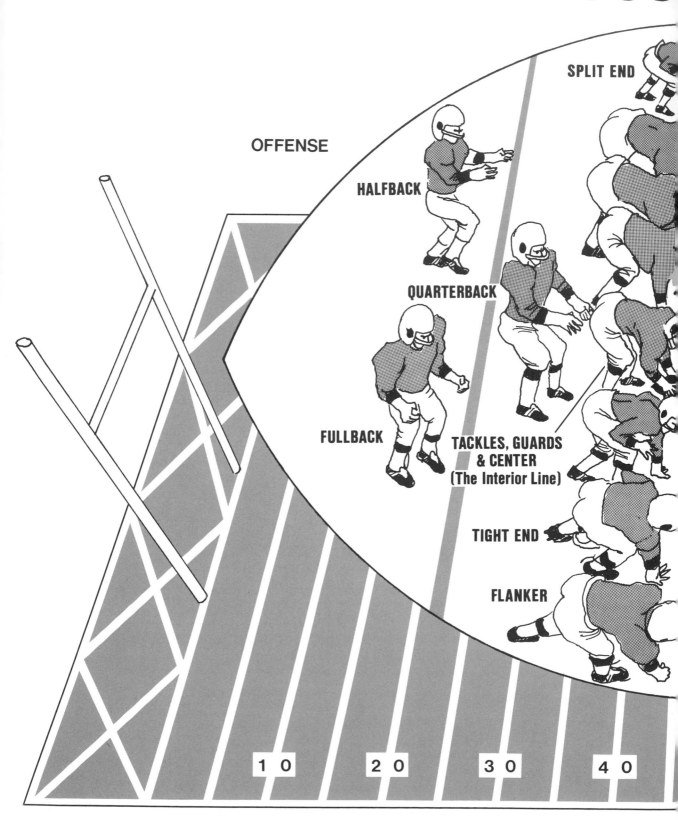

FOO

SPLIT END

OFFENSE

HALFBACK

QUARTERBACK

FULLBACK

TACKLES, GUARDS
& CENTER
(The Interior Line)

TIGHT END

FLANKER

1 0     2 0     3 0     4 0

**ALL**

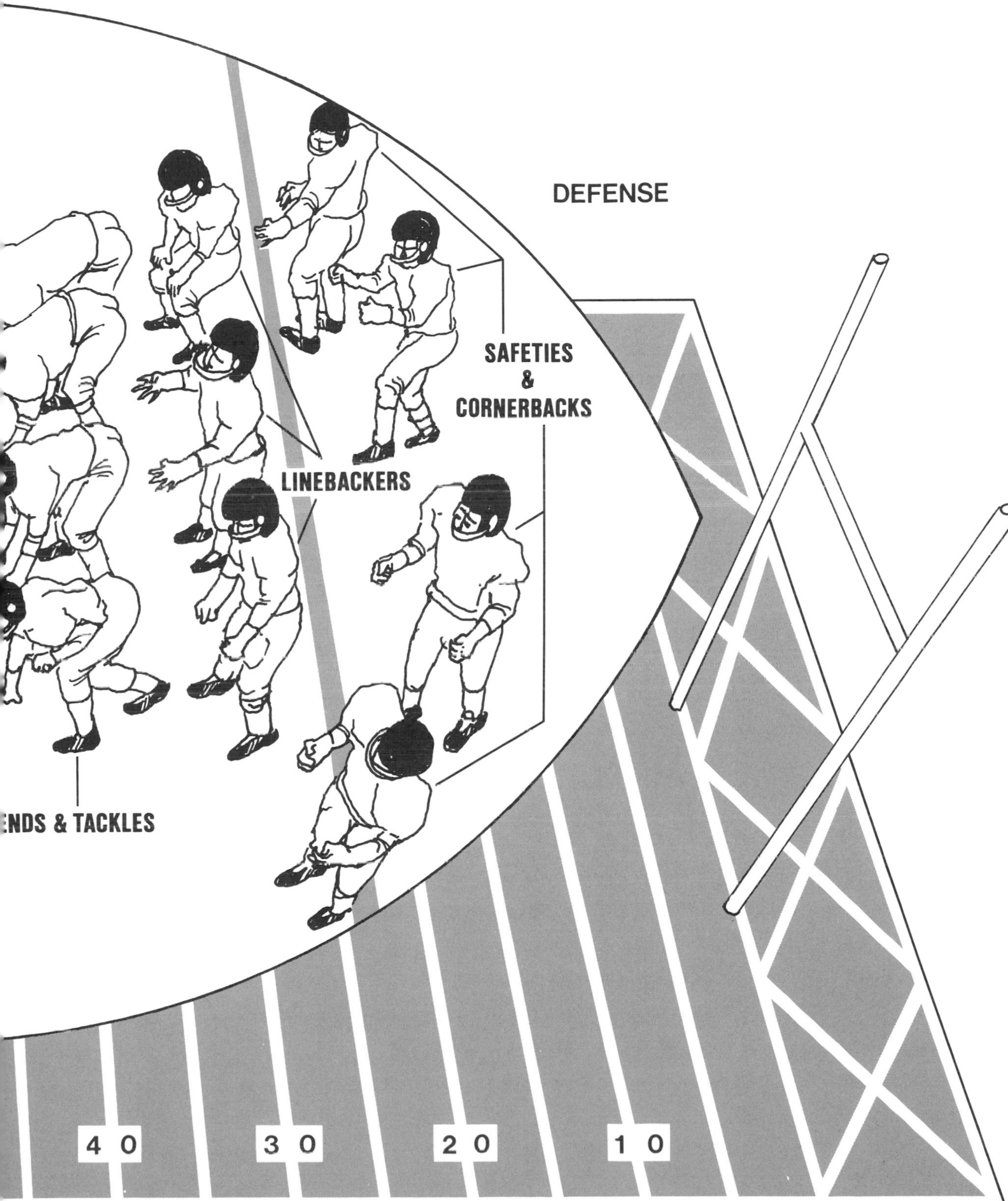

DEFENSE

SAFETIES
&
CORNERBACKS

LINEBACKERS

ENDS & TACKLES

40    30    20    10

# FOOTBALL REFEREE SIGNALS

**FIRST DOWN**

**HOLDING**

**DELAY OF GAME**

**OFFSIDES**

**TOUCHDOWN OR FIELD GOAL**

**ILLEGAL MOTION**

**SAFETY**

**ILLEGAL PROCEDURE**

**INTERFERENCE**

**CLIPPING**

**DEAD BALL**

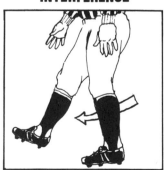

**ROUGHING THE KICKER**

COMMON PENALTIES:

CLIPPING: When, from behind a player throws his body across the leg or legs of a player not carrying the ball (except on the line of scrimmage). This is a personal foul. The penalty is fifteen yards from the point where the infraction occurred.

DELAY OF GAME: When the offensive team does not put the ball in play within twenty-five seconds after the referee has started play. Five-yard penalty.

ILLEGAL PROCEDURE: When the offensive team does not have seven men on the line or if an offensive player moves forward before the center snaps the ball. This results in a five-yard penalty.

INTERFERENCE: If either the pass receiver or the pass defender is tackled or blocked after the ball has been thrown, or before either has a chance to catch the ball. If the defender interferes, the offensive team receives a first down at the point of the foul. If the receiver interferes, the offensive team is penalized fifteen yards plus the loss of down.

HOLDING: If an offensive player *blocks*—seizes or obstructs the way of the opponent—with his hands away from his body or stops a player by some method other than a legal block. (Blocking must be done while facing the man, or from the side. The most common method of blocking is to stop the forward motion of an opposing player with a shoulder.) *Defensive holding* is called if a defender grabs an offensive player and holds him. The penalty is fifteen yards for offensive holding or five yards for defensive holding.

OFFSIDES: If a player crosses the line of scrimmage before the ball is in play, his team is penalized five yards.

BACKFIELD IN MOTION: When one or more offensive backs move forward before the ball is snapped. The penalty is five yards.

ILLEGAL MOTION: Illegal movement by an offensive player. All offensive players must come to a full stop for at least one second before the ball is snapped.

ROUGHING THE KICKER: Unnecessarily hitting or tackling the kicker after he has kicked the ball is illegal; the penalty is 15 yards and the ball remains in possession of the kicking team.

## Basketball

PLAYING SURFACE:   A hard, level court made of wood.

PLAYING TIME:   High school basketball games last thirty-two minutes. They consist of two sixteen-minute halves or four eight-minute quarters. Teams rest for one minute at the end of the first and third quarters and for ten minutes between halves. If the score of a basketball game is tied when the time runs out, the teams play a three-minute overtime period.

THE CLOCK:   During the game, the clock is stopped when an official indicates that a player has broken a rule, a player is injured, an official needs additional time to get the ball back into play, or a team asks for a time-out. Each team is permitted five time-outs during a game.

TEAMS:   A basketball team has five players who work together to score baskets and to stop the other team from scoring. The team trying to score is the *offense.* The other team is the *defense.* The *center,* or *pivot player,* is generally the tallest player on most teams and plays nearest the basket. Two *forwards,* also called *cornermen,* play near the corners of the court, but may move in toward the basket at any time. *Guards* are usually the shortest but the quickest players and the best ball handlers. They play toward the middle of the court (outside the free-throw circle). The *point guard* directs the team. All offensive players try to score with the ball. When playing defense, players try to prevent their opponents from scoring.

SCORING:   There are two ways to score points in a basketball game. A successful basket, called a *field goal,* counts two points. Any player may attempt to score a field goal from anywhere on the court. A successful *free throw,* or *foul shot,* counts one point. The fouled player shoots from behind the free-throw line. He has ten seconds to shoot, during which time no other player may enter the free-throw lane until the ball hits the basket or the backboard.

PLAY:   A basketball game starts with a referee tossing the ball into the air above the centers, who jump up and try to tap it to one of their teammates. Once a team gets the ball, the players move it toward the opponent's basket and try to score. The player who has the ball may advance it by (1) bouncing it along the floor with one hand (called *dribbling*), (2) passing it to a teammate, or (3) shooting it at the basket. When a player misses a basket, both teams try to catch the ball on the *rebound* when it bounces from the rim of the basket or off the backboard. After a team scores, a member of the opposing team throws the ball to a teammate into the court from behind the basket.

FOULS: Both offense and defense players may commit fouls. The most common type of foul is the *personal foul*. It occurs when a player pushes, charges, trips, or comes in contact with an opponent. When a defensive player commits a personal foul, the fouled player receives either one or two free throws after the opposing team has committed five fouls during a quarter. He gets one if he was not shooting when fouled. He also gets one if he was shooting and his shot was good. A player gets two free throws if he was shooting when fouled and his shot was unsuccessful. When an offensive player commits a personal foul, his team loses possession of the ball. A player is automatically removed from the game after he has committed five fouls. After a team commits five fouls, the fouled player receives a *bonus shot* if he makes his foul shot.

A *technical foul* may be called by an official when a player delays the game, a team takes too many time-outs, a player enters or leaves the court illegally, or a player or coach shows unsportsmanlike conduct. When a team is charged with a technical foul, the opposing team receives one free throw and gets possession of the ball.

VIOLATIONS: These are infractions of the rules that result in a team's losing possession of the ball or in a jump ball. A team loses the ball for such violations as traveling, double dribbling, kicking the ball, causing the ball to go out of bounds, and for spending three seconds in the lane.

TRAVELING: When a player walks or runs while holding the ball.

DOUBLE DRIBBLE: When a player stops dribbling, then starts again. Also, when a player bounces the ball with both hands.

BALL OUT OF BOUNDS: When the player controlling the ball touches or crosses an end line or sideline or when the ball leaves the court.

TIME RESTRICTIONS: There's a five-second rule for getting the ball into the court and a ten-second rule for getting it across the *time line* (midcourt line). In addition, an offensive player cannot stand in his team's free-throw lane for three or more seconds with or without the ball.

FORWARD

FORWARD

GUARD

GUARD

CENTER

CENTER

FORWARD

FORWARD

GUARD

GUARD

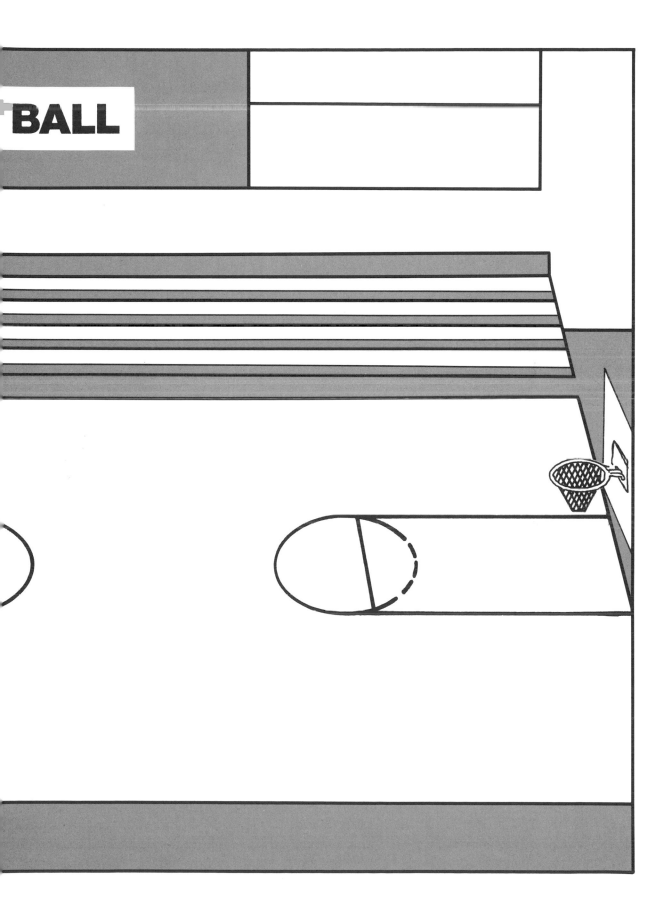

# BASKETBALL
# REFEREE SIGNALS

**HOLDING**

**TECHNICAL FOUL**

**POINTS SCORED**

**START THE CLOCK**

**STOP THE CLOCK**

**STOP CLOCK FOR FOUL**

**PUSH OR CHARGING**

**BLOCKING**

**BONUS SITUATION**

**TRAVELING**

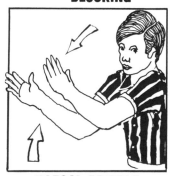
**ILLEGAL DRIBBLE**

**3 SECOND VIOLATION**

HOLDING: Personal contact with an opponent which interferes with freedom of movement.

BLOCKING: An illegal play which impedes the progress of an opponent.

At some schools there are sports that never seem to get the attention they deserve. After football and basketball season SPIRIT just seems to fade. Yet, spring sports are every bit as exciting as fall or winter sports. And for an athlete, there's no such thing as a minor sport. Do talk to the coaches about the spring sports at your school. Ask how your squad may support the team. Then, take some time out and learn the basic rules of each sport so you can go right out and cheer! (For any sport but tennis.)

# Planning Innovative Pep Rallies

There's nothing like an innovative pep rally for stimulating school spirit. A successful rally can create a feeling of unity among the student body which is guaranteed to bring everyone to the game and motivate a sports team.

Effective pep rallies depend on the quality of the work put into them, the NCA will tell you. Without planning, a rally will surely fall flat, and you would have only yourself and your squad to blame for how you handled it.

## Getting Organized

It's easy to come up with a winner with these four tips from the NCA:

1.  BE PREPARED.   When there's a whole new school year coming up, you'd be smart to meet with the administration to discuss squad objectives and plans for the coming year. It's also wise to schedule monthly meetings with administrators to clear any new ideas as they come up (unless your advisor prefers to act as the spokesperson for the squad). Also, introduce yourself to those who will be involved with your rallies—the band director, the custodian, and the coaches. It helps if you can create a feeling of goodwill between them and your squad.

2.  GET ORGANIZED.   Keep a spirit book, jotting down new ideas and themes that might be forgotten. You should also include the ideas that did not work, so you won't make the mistake of trying them again.

The key to a successful pep rally is organization. At least two weeks before the rally you need to agree on a date, time, and place. Consult with the head coaches and consider their time preferences for the rally so that the coaches and teams can attend. Show your interest in the school's athletic program by including all seasonal sports —both girls' and boys'—in the rally. Next, appoint a rally chairman. You can suggest a theme for the rally, but do let the chairman and his or her committee plan the agenda. After all, it's up to them to come up with activities, posters, and slogans that fit the theme.

3.  DELEGATE RESPONSIBILITIES.  The rally chairman will be overwhelmed by the size of the job ahead, unless he or she sets up committees. Someone should be asked to plan the skit, then cast it so the participants can practice. Another squad member can set up a committee to handle publicity and promotion. Let a third person be in charge of the location and how it looks, both before and after the rally. Finally, someone should follow up with a suggestion box survey or discussion of the rally with friends.

4.  HOLD A DRESS REHEARSAL.  The best pep rallies last no more than twenty minutes. After that, one tends to drag. You want to keep things moving, so time the rally, and make sure it's always going strong. If it drags at rehearsal, it will drag at the real thing, but you'll have time to whip it into shape. Without a rehearsal, you'll never know until it's too late to act.

If you're hunting for ways to put more pep into your rallies, here are some:

• Use your imagination. Grab everyone's attention with something offbeat. You might, for example, black out the lights in the gym after everyone's seated, play rock music over the public address system, or set off the fire alarm (with the administration's approval, of course) and have the rally outside when everyone gets there.

• Add humor.

• Involve as many students as you can. The larger the group, the more ideas they'll generate. Also, remember that people generally will support something they've helped to create.

• Have a different group prepare the skit for each rally.

• Experiment with different kinds of rallies. If you usually

meet in the gym, consider holding a rally on the school roof, or meeting at a mall, or on a road-blocked street where you can include the public. (Then remember to gear the rally to both students and fans.) Avoid always gathering at the same time and the same place. And don't hold a rally when it's not needed.

To be a real spirit booster, a pep rally needs

- The Pledge of Allegiance and/or the National Anthem (FIRST!)
- Cheers. Open with a favorite and sprinkle the rest of the best throughout the rally.
- Brief talks by those coaches and players who have been invited to speak.
- The school song and/or fight song.
- A short skit, competitive cheering, or stunts.
- A new cheer, information about game rules, or a quick word on sportsmanship and fair play.

Vary the routine to keep your rallies in motion. And don't forget to check the public address system and microphone *before* the rally, or you could be embarrassed.

## Time Line

The ideal place to introduce a new cheer is at a rally. Ditto a flyer with the words and hand it out at the door. When you're ready, explain the cheer's purpose. Then show the cheer and put SPIRIT into it! Stress the timing and wording

Try something different.

To have a bonfire you need permission from your city.

before inviting everyone to join in. Praise them again and again. It's a good idea to have a new cheer printed on the back of the game program, too, to refresh people's memories. But it isn't wise to introduce more than two new shouts at once.

## Sign Up

Don't wait until the last minute to make your posters and signs—plan ahead. Gather as many interested people as you need and have them put their ideas on posters. Then decorate the halls with the week's theme. While you're painting, make a sign for the bus in which the team will be riding to an away game. Staying at home, you could decorate their locker room or build a huge sign for them to run through as they charge onto the field. Another nice touch would be to personalize signs with player's name, picture, or number and tape them on their lockers the night before the game—with the coaches' approval, of course. (Some cheerleaders also like to leave a quick energy treat.)

In planning for your posters, these are the materials the NCA says you need: Tempera paint; wide-tip magic markers; paintbrushes; pencils; erasers; coffee cans and stir sticks for mixing paint; metal ruler; masking tape, Scotch tape, stencils, or lettering book; pictures of the rival mascot; butcher paper or newsprint roll.

Remember the coach.

"Kiss St. John's Goodbye."

## POSTERS

Before beginning to paint the poster itself, read over the wording you've planned and be sure it's creative! Then eliminate any unnecessary words. First rule of thumb is that the fewer the words, the bigger and bolder the impact. Experiment with different designs on a scratch sheet until you come up with a strong composition. Then doublecheck that your poster makes a dynamic message.

Letters should be LARGE, CLEAN CUT, and of no more than two BOLD colors, preferably those of your school. The NCA points out your signs will be easier to read from a distance when all letters are colored in, and they don't have fancy borders. In addition, it suggests simple line lettering be

enhanced by adding something to the end of each brush stroke. But don't add too much, or the poster will be hard to read.

If you don't have a steady hand, use a stencil and paint over each letter. Remove the stencil carefully so you don't smudge the letters when you pick it up.

You can hang your posters and signs almost anywhere—

- From the ceiling
- In the classroom
- On columns, around poles

- From the bleachers
- In the locker room
- All over the halls

Another nifty place to hang signs . . . at the players' homes. In the Southwest, the houses of the very best players are "wrapped" with signs and toilet tissue the night before the game. And it's truly a compliment.

## Skits

Skits liven up pep rallies and create more spirit for the game. Good skits are both entertaining and meaningful, but the best ones are short and to the point. This, of course, takes planning. To start, the NCA suggests you look around for ideas. Take a look at

- Historical people and events.

- Famous places all over the world.

- Holidays.

- Television shows.

- Current events.

- Fairy tales.

- Your mascot. Mascots come in all sizes, shapes, and forms. For example, a student in costume, a young child wearing a cheerleading uniform, or even a live animal. Whatever your mascot, it should add to your squad's presentation, not detract from it.

There are many different types of mascots.

Below are some NCA points that add up to the best skits.

- Always use good taste in selecting a skit's theme and in writing it. Don't offend anyone.

- Sandwich in as many people as you can, including faculty and coaches.

- Props are essential. Though they don't have to be fancy, they should be funny. You want people to laugh.

- A skit should last five to eight minutes, never any longer.

- Practice. And practice some more.


## NCA Skits

Here are some skits the NCA has written. You can use these or read them, then bring your own ideas to life. Fill in the blanks with the name of your rival team in the following skits.

### The Doctor's Office

*(Two or more* Cheerleaders *enter the* Doctor's office carrying their Mascot, *who seems sick.* Nurse *is standing at a table in the middle of the floor.)*

*First Cheerleader:* Nurse, nurse! We must see the doctor in a hurry! It's an emergency! We have a big game tonight, and something's wrong with our Mascot.

*Second Cheerleader:* He just doesn't seem to have any more spirit. We thought maybe the doctor could operate on him or something, and give him some spirit. We're playing those _____ _____ tonight and we need as much spirit as we can get.

*Nurse:* We're awfully booked up. The doctor can see your mascot on July nineteenth.

*First Cheerleader:* The game's tonight *(sob).* We need the doctor today!

*Nurse:* Well, I'll try to reach him and see what he's got to say. *(Beeps the* Doctor. *Everyone paces. Finally, telephone rings.)* Hello, doctor, this is your nurse at the office. Yes sir, doctor, I know you're on vacation, but we've got an emergency. The Hometown Mascot needs a spirit operation before the big game tonight. He'll have a hard time beating the _____ _____ without spirit. Okay, I'll get everything ready. *(She hangs up phone.)* The doctor said he'll be here as soon as he gets his golfball out of the creek.

*Doctor (Entering with golf bag over his shoulder. Sternly):* I haven't finished a golf game in twenty years. Up on the table. *(Hometown Mascot slowly sits on the edge of the table.* Doctor *begins to examine him.)* What's your problem? Oh, forget it. Say, "ah."

*Hometown Mascot (Opening his mouth):* Ah.
*(Doctor then hits him on the knee to check his reflexes. When he hits his knee, his arm jumps up. When he twists his arm, his leg jumps up.* Doctor *is amazed.)*

*Doctor:* Weird, weird. Yes, you're sick all right. We'll have to operate immediately. Lie down. *(Doctor puts sheet over patient.)* I'll have to call in the rest of my surgery team. *(He whistles them into the room. Four* Assistants *stand at the surgery table, one at each end and on both sides of the* Doctor.*)* At right oxygen tank will be Tanker Thompson. Playing at left stomach pump is Earl Esophagus. At quarter-table is Scissors Smith. And playing at left end-tern is Dirty Utensils. *(When introduced, each* Assistant *raises a hand and is cheered by the* Cheerleaders.*)* May I have my operating gloves, please. *(Nurse puts two baseball mitts on his hands.)* Okay, here's the game plan. *(The* Assistants *lean over the table toward the* Doctor. *He acts as if he is quarterback in a huddle.)* Now you open up a big hole in the middle. Then *you* take out the right side. Then we run our blood pressure option play: *You* hand the scissors off to me and I'll go right up the middle. Get it?

*Assistants:* Got it!

*Doctor:* Good! Ready? Break! *(All clap hands like they're breaking out of a huddle. Then the* Doctor *talks to the* Mascot.) Now we're going to operate so we can give you more spirit. And if you're a good patient, I'll give you a surprise. The latest thing in hospital toys. *(Doctor gets out a doll and gives it to the* Mascot.) It's a doctor doll. You must wind it up and it operates on batteries. *(The* Mascot *acts happy.)* Now be still and shut up!

*(The operation begins. The* Assistants *help by handing the* Doctor *a crowbar, a water hose, a hot water bottle, a pipe wrench, etc., or anything that would appear strange for a doctor to use.)*

*First Assistant:* Has he got a chance, doctor?

*Doctor:* Looks pretty dim right now. I just don't know for sure.

*Second Assistant   (Holding* Mascot's *hand):* His blood pressure is slowly decreasing.

*First Cheerleader   (Pleading):* Oh, doctor, is he going to make it? Is he going to make it?

*Doctor:*   Well, I'm no Marcus Welby, but I'll do the best I can. Like I always say, "Visit your doctor once a year, even if it kills you!" *(Assistants continue to hand array of tools to the doctor.)* Everybody look here. *(They gather around.)* That's his liver!

*Third Assistant:*   How can you tell?

*Doctor:*   It has gravy and onions around it! *(Operation continues.)* Yeah, this Hometown Mascot definitely needs some school spirit if he is going to win the game tonight. It's almost time for the final step in this operation. Bring the spirit stick to me. I'm sure this will really help him! *(An* Assistant *hands a spirit stick to the* Doctor. *Or it could be poured from a spirit jar or something similar into the* Mascot.) Here goes. *(Doctor pretends to put the spirit stick into the* Mascot *but actually slips it under the sheet and places it on the table. Then acts out the rest of the operation.)* That's it. Your mascot has enough spirit now to beat the _____ _____.

*(The* Mascot *begins to stir, then jumps up and starts a spirit chant, which the entire student body follows.)*

*Mascot:*   We've got spirit. We've got spirit. Everybody. *(Repeat chant several times with everybody joining in. The rhythm for this particular chant is:*

<pre>
       1     2     3     4     1     2     3     4
   We've got spir-it. We've got spirit. Everybody.)
</pre>

### The Defeated Mascots' Wax Museum

*(Carnival Barker or* Caller *with cane and top hat stands in front of the "Defeated Mascots' Wax Museum." The museum has a big sign in the front with its name. Carnival music plays in background.)*

*Barker:* Ladies and gentlemen, step right up and see a most extraordinary museum. See the displays and exact replicas of all the teams defeated by those mighty Hometown Mascots. Yes, folks, this is the Defeated Mascots' Wax Museum. Incredible! Unbelievable! And all for one thin dime. Yes, that's right, just one thin dime. The show starts in five minutes, so get your ticket. *(Four* Customers *who have gathered enter museum. Inside the museum three former* Mascots *who have been defeated by the Hometown Mascot stand in stiff positions like wax figures. Each is dressed in own mascot uniform.)* Please walk this way. *(He walks with a limp or weird twist in his legs. The* Customers *walk the same way he does. They go to the* First Mascot *and gaze at him.)*

*First Customer:* Oh, what does this sign say?

*Second Customer: (Reading sign in front of* Mascots): It says, "Insert twenty-five cents and hear the voice of the defeated mascot. Hear the story of how this mascot lost to the Hometown Mascots. Get it straight from the horse's mouth."

*Third Customer:* That sounds neat! Let's put a quarter in each mascot and hear their stories.

*(He puts quarter in* First Mascot. *When each* Mascot *says his individual poem, he should try to act it out so it can be funny. [New poems can be written if more mascots are needed to make skit longer.]* First Mascot *slowly comes alive and humorously acts out poem, then returns to stiff position.)*

*First Mascot:* I ran on the field like an ace.
    But right off I caught a shoe in my face.
    They grabbed my big toe,
    Swung it 'round and let it go;
    Then knocked my poor head into space. *(He gazes into sky.)*

*Fourth Customer:* Ah! Too bad. Let's see how it went for this next mascot. *(Puts quarter in* Second Mascot *as all gather around him.)*

*Second Mascot:* We used to be known as Big Red,
Till those [Hometown] Mascots filled us with lead.
They slapped us with crud;
Then drug us through mud.
They really put the hurt on our heads.

*First Customer:* Better luck next time. *(Customers go to next* Mascot *and put in quarter.)* Wonder what this one has to say?

*Third Mascot:* At the game when I started to block,
I got hit on the head with a rock.
My feet got a blister *(Holds up bare foot);*
I got knocked in the kisser.
And they threw away the key to this lock. *(He is draped with locks and chains.)*

*Second Customer:* Poor little thing. Come on, let's try this mascot. *(Goes to next* Mascot *and puts in quarter.)*

*Fourth Mascot:* I'm quickly becoming antique,
And my arms are starting to squeak,
'Cause they ripped off my shoulder,
Put my body under this boulder. *(He is lying under a big rock),*
And I've been here crying for a week! *(He begins to cry.)*

*(Customers go to last* Mascot, *who is covered by a bed sheet.* Man *is working on the last* Mascot, *the one the Hometown Mascots will be playing in the up-coming game.)*

*Third Customer* *(Talking to* Man *who is working on* Mascot*):* What have we got here? Haven't you finished this mascot yet?

*Worker:* No. This is the _____ Mascot. He'll be playing those mighty (Hometown) Mascots this next game. There's no way that he can beat them, so I thought I'd go ahead and put him on display. *(Fixes something on* Mascot's *head.)* There, he's all finished. Would you like to hear his voice?

*All Customers:* Yeah! Yeah!

*Fourth Customer:* Let's hear how he lost to the (Hometown) Mascots!

*(Worker removes veil and puts in quarter. Fifth Mascot's clothes are in shreds; he might wear bandages and some tape. He should appear to be in very bad physical shape.)*

*Fifth Mascot:*   My teammates called me Billy the Kid,
'Cause I stayed for the game while they hid.
But I should have got lost,
'Cause I got stomped on and tossed.
So what you see is what they did. *(Said in Flip Wilson voice. All laugh at* Mascot, *then exit.)*


## The Wounded Mascots' Hospital

*(Five former* Mascots *whom the Hometown Mascot has defeated enter all beaten up; wearing bandages, ace wraps, on crutches, with towels, etc.; moaning with illness and pain as they enter their hospital room after having lunch.)*

*First Mascot:*   Oh, that food in the hospital cafeteria gets worse every meal. I just can't take any more.

*Second Mascot:*   Yeah. You know it's important not to waste any food, but their idea of being thrifty is to serve the dishwater in cups and call it lemonade.

*Third Mascot:* And that cured ham was terrible. I wonder what sickness it had before they cured it.

*Fourth Mascot   (Points an accusing finger at all of them):* And which one of you guys put spiders in the Jell-O? I wanna know right now.

*All Mascots:*   Ooooooohhhh!

*(They hold their stomachs as they go to their respective beds, sleeping bags, or beach towels and pillows, and all lie down moaning; above each bed is a sign giving the name of each team and* Mascot. Doctor *enters and blows whistle hanging around his neck.* Nurse *is standing beside him.)*

*Doctor:*   Okay. Quiet. No more complaining. I'm your doctor for this week.

*First Mascot:*   I thought you kinda resembled Marcus Welby. *(*Mascots *laugh.)*

*Second Mascot:*   I was thinking more on the line of Florence Nightingale.

*Doctor:*   Cut it out before I send you back to the cafeteria.

*All Mascots:*   Oh no! Oh no! *(Expressing horror at* Doctor's suggestion)

*Doctor:*   By the way, what are all you mascots doing here in the hospital anyway?

*Third Mascot:*   Oh, Doctor, we're all in bad shape. Everyone of us has a broken arm or leg, or some other kind of pain.

*Nurse:*   How come?

*Fourth Mascot:*   We've all had to play those (Hometown) Mascots this year in football. They're so rough and tough that they beat us all up, and that's why we're here in the hospital.

*First Mascot:*   I remember in our game, their fullback came up to me during the first quarter and said, "You're number one on my 'hit parade.'" Then he hit me. Whop! *(Swings his fist like a boxer, then acts like he got knocked out.)*

*Second Mascot   (Reaching for* Nurse): Nurse, nurse, those (Hometown) Mascots nearly killed me. I'm about to die.

*Nurse:*   Well hurry up. We've got a waiting line out in the parking lot.

*Doctor:*   I had better give the rest of you guys a checkup to see what's ailing you. *(Goes to* Third Mascot.) *Okay, what's your problem?*

*(Each wounded* Mascot *could say lines pertaining to himself about how badly he was beaten by the* Hometown Mascots; *for example:* Eagles—"They pulled all my feathers out, and now I'm bald." Bulldogs—"They took away my flea collar, and now I'm itching myself to death." Mustangs—"They put me in a barn, crammed alfalfa down my throat, and now I've got hay breath.")*

*Third Mascot:*   In our game we had a huge pile of people right in the middle of the field. A million of these (Hometown) Mascots tackled me. There was a hand in my mouth, so I bit it off. Then when we all got up, I found that I had bitten off my own hand. *(Holds it up.* Doctor *shakes his head and goes to next* Mascot.)

*Doctor:*   What's wrong with you?

*Fourth Mascot   (Crying):* You see, I'm the quarterback for our team, and those (Hometown) Mascots caught every-thing I threw. I couldn't complete a pass all night. I got mad and threw my helmet down and even it got intercepted. *(Doctor shakes his head and goes to next Mascot.)*

*Fifth Mascot  (With his head inside his jacket as though he were headless):* Besides getting my head knocked off by those (Hometown) Mascots, an alligator ate off one of my legs.

*Doctor:*  Which one?

*Fifth Mascot:*  Don't know. All those alligators look the same to me.

*(Telephone rings and* Nurse *picks it up.)*

*Nurse:*  Hello. This is the hospital for wounded mascots. *(Pauses for second.)* Doctor, it's for you.

*Doctor:*  Hello. *(He listens intently.)* You don't say. *(Pauses.)* You don't say. *(Pauses.)* You don't say. *(Hangs up.)*

*All Mascots:*  Who was it?

*Doctor:*  He didn't say. No, it was the hospital reporter at the football game between the _____ _____ and the Hometown Mascots. He says there are a lot of casual-ties. Nearly everybody on the team got hurt.

*Second Mascot:*  Which mascots got hurt so bad, the _____ _____ or the (Hometown) Mascots?

*Doctor:*  I'm not sure, we'll just have to wait and see.

*Nurse  (Disgusted):* Looks like we're gonna have some more wounded mascots lying around everywhere. *(Ambulance siren is heard outside.)*

*Doctor:*  Here they are now.

*(Hometown Mascots drag in the* Rival Mascots, *clasp hands above heads like they conquered them, then wipe off hands.)*

*First Hometown Mascot:*  Doc, I hope you have enough room to take care of these _____ _____. We were just gonna beat 'em up a little bit, but once we got started, we just couldn't stop.

*Second Hometown Mascot:*  Yeah. Hope you got enough Band-Aids for these critters.

*Doctor:* We'll manage to take care of 'em somehow. *(All wounded* Mascots *are trembling or peeking from under the covers.)*

*Third Hometown Mascot (As they exit):* Oh yes, one more thing. Get some more rooms ready 'cause next week we'll be bringing in some more wounded critters.


## The Hometown Carnival

*(Scene opens with four imaginary booths at a carnival. Each booth has in it something different to do to other* Mascots. *The first three may be any* Mascot *desired, but the* Fourth Mascot *should be opponent mascot of up-coming game. On each booth is a sign naming booth. Three* Hometown Cheerleaders *enter the carnival.)*

*First Cheerleader.* This is the neatest carnival we've ever had here. I just love all the rides. Everything is so much fun.

*Second Cheerleader. (Dizzy from the last ride):* I don't know. That roller coaster still has me going in circles. I'm still a little woozy. *(Stumbles around like he's sick.)* My stomach hasn't felt this bad since the time I ate those five dog-food sandwiches.

*Third Cheerleader:* Oh look, everybody! The midway! This is my favorite part of the carnival. We've just got to go to every booth. Maybe we'll win a stuffed toy.

*Second Cheerleader:* You can have me. After eight hot dogs, five candy apples, and sixteen Dilly bars, I'm about as stuffed as anything you'll win here. *(Holds stomach.)*

*First Cheerleader:* This first booth looks like fun. It's the "Baseball Throw." *(Reading sign on booth.)* All we have to do is knock over those stupid-looking clowns. *(Have two* Mascots *dressed funny standing at the back of the imaginary booth. A* Cheerleader *picks up imaginary baseball to throw.)*

*Second Cheerleader:* Oh, I can do this one. *(Winds up like a pitcher, throws "baseball," and knocks the* Mascots *down.)* Did you see that curve ball? *(Bragging.)* I used to play on the same team with Peanuts and Charlie Brown.

*Third Cheerleader* *(Noticing next booth):* This booth should be fun. It's called "Pin the Tail on the Coyote." This is my specialty. Just watch.

*(Mascot in booth stands in a chair and howls like a coyote. Two of the Cheerleaders blindfold the other one, who walks around seemingly lost in darkness. She approaches the howling coyote. The coyote jumps and lets out a big howl when she pins the tail on him. He runs around howling, then exits.)*

*First Cheerleader* *(Going to next booth):* Here's the booth I like. It's the "Hawks Shooting Gallery." All we have to do is shoot those weird hawks flying around back there.

*(Two Mascots in booth flap their arms like wings, and move from one side of the booth to the other, as though they are tied to a conveyor belt or a moving track. The Cheerleaders shoot the hawks, who fall dead. You might rather have ducks, so Mascots could waddle along. It might be funnier.)*

*Second Cheerleader* *(As they all go to next booth):* Check this next booth out. It should be the most fun of all. We're all going to have to try it.

*Third Cheerleader:* What is it?

*First Cheerleader* "It's the _____ _____ Sledge-hammer" up there. *(Rival Mascots' Coach is sitting at the top of a ladder. Someone Else is at the bottom of the ladder with a cream pie in hand.)* If we hit this thing hard enough with a sledgehammer, we can knock that pie into his face. Come on, let's try it. *(She hits ground with imaginary hammer, then Person with the Pie goes up toward the Coach but then comes down without hitting him. The Cheerleaders voice their disappointment.)* I guess I'm not strong enough. Why don't you try?

*Second Cheerleader:* I can do it. Just watch this. *(Takes hammer and hits ground. Person goes up ladder again but still doesn't hit the Coach. Everyone is disappointed again.)* I guess I'm not strong enough either. It's your turn.

*Third Cheerleader* *(Taking hammer and spitting in hands to get a good grip):* I hope I can do it. There's nothing I'd rather do than knock that pie in the _____ _____ coach's face. *(Hits ground, but the same thing happens: no pie in the face. They are even more disappointed.)*

*First Cheerleader:*   What are we going to do? We're just not strong enough. We've got to have bigger muscles.

*Second Cheerleader:*   Maybe we could get one of our team captains to try. I'm sure one of them is strong enough.

*Third Cheerleader:*   There's Tommy over there. Let's get him to try.

*All:*   Tommy! Tommy!

*(Tommy comes over to them.)*

*First Cheerleader:*   You've just got to hit this thing hard enough so that the pie will hit the _____ _____ coach in the face.

*Tommy:*   My pleasure. *(Takes the hammer.)* This is just exactly what our team is going to do to those _____ _____ tonight at the game.

*(Hits ground, and the* Rival Mascots' Coach *gets the pie in his face. Do take precautions to prevent mishaps. Talk to the principal or a popular teacher about playing the role of the Rival Mascots' Coach. This will help to make it funnier. But be sure the person understands exactly what will happen. You don't want anyone to be upset.)*

# Controlling the Crowd

Controlling any crowd, especially an excited one, is perhaps the most difficult task of a cheerleader. However, knowing the secrets of effective crowd control can make it a lot easier.

Start with winning the respect and support of the fans by looking good and putting your skills to work. It's simply a matter of being aware that how you act toward people often influences the way they react to you. *Skill* is the key factor. Here's a guide to all the skills you need, from the NCA, who has been pinpointing the problems of cheerleading for years.

1. BE PREPARED, ALERT, AND WELL-ORGANIZED. Be on your best behavior to gain the respect of the crowd and win their support. Besides, there's no time to fool around —your job requires your complete attention. So watch the game instead of your friends, even if your current interest happens to be in the stands with someone else. When you follow the game, you'll know which cheers are appropriate. It helps to tape a list of cheers and chants on the inside of your megaphone for immediate access to yells you might otherwise forget. Some head cheerleaders list them in categories, such as fight cheers, offensive cheers, defensive cheers, and boogie cheers.

2. BE SENSITIVE TO YOUR CROWD. It's important to know what is happening on the field, but also be aware of what's going on in the stands. If it appears that the crowd is "fired up" and ready, then it's the cheerleader's responsibility to begin an appropriate cheer. A cheerleader's primary job is leadership, and if you don't take

217

the role, a crowd may take it upon themselves to lead their own cheers—which may or may not be in the best of taste!

On the other hand, no one says you have to cheer all the time. There are instances when doing so is clearly inappropriate. If your team is losing and the crowd isn't cheering, do not try to force the issue by persisting in doing one chant after another. Be sensitive to the crowd and to the situation.

3. BE ASSERTIVE IN COMMUNICATING WITH THE CROWD. You can be assertive in a most graceful and tactful manner. A crowd should look to you for leadership. You already know that good techniques, such as strong, definite motions are the most effective ways to lead your crowd. Visual cues are another excellent communication tool. For example, the head cheerleader may hold up two fingers, then one finger before using a cutoff signal to show when to quit yelling. Vocal cues are effective, too. Between phrases of chants is the best time to shout: "Two more times, let's really yell," or something similar. As for megaphone and microphone technique:

Use good megaphone techniques.

- Do speak clearly and loudly.

- Don't scream into the microphone.

- Don't wave or swing either around.

- Don't throw a megaphone.

4. SELECT EFFECTIVE CHEERS AND CHANTS. You set the mood of your fans with the type of cheers and chants you use. If you chant, "We want blood, we want blood," the NCA points out you just might get it. Stay away from chants like this one and channel the crowd's energy constructively.

5. BE EFFECTIVE IN CONTROLLING DISPLAYS OF POOR SPORTSMANSHIP. Booing and harassment by the crowd are two problems that spiritleaders must learn to deal with. It's up to a cheerleader to handle poor sportsmanship before it becomes a problem. Therefore, no matter how unfair you may feel the situation is, it's up to you to discourage it.

- Wave off booing at the first sign. If you find the fans waving back at you as they continue booing . . .

- Divert their attention by starting their favorite cheer.

- Signal the band director to strike up the school fight song, or have the drummer accompany a chant with a drum roll.

## Promote Sportsmanship

It goes without saying, whenever two sports teams meet, one will win, the other lose! Accepting this fact makes losing less frustrating without reducing one's pride. Do be a sport and teach others to be good sports too, by making them aware that a good sport . . .

- Never boos an official or a player. Instead, accepts the decisions of the game officials as final, without expressing disapproval or encouraging retaliating rough play.

- Cheers positively.

- Appreciates a good play, no matter who makes it.

- Applauds players who make good plays or show good sportsmanship.

- Strives to win fairly and knows the values of fair play.

- Supports the team enthusiastically but with consideration and respect for others—whether winning or losing.

- Respects all involved in the sport—officials, coaches, players, managers, announcers, the student body, and fans.

- Doesn't try to rattle an opponent.

- Knows the rules of the sport.

- Is modest in victory and gracious in defeat—never offering an excuse.

## Grin and Bear It

There are people who take great pleasure in trying to distract, frustrate, and embarrass cheerleaders. Sometimes they make you the target of their jokes. When unruly people harass you, ignore them. When they see they can't get to you, the fun is often gone, and they generally quit trying.

Never let anyone drive you to despair. When you've had it with a certain person, resist the temptation to be rude, simply follow the crowd, and put physical distance between the two of you once the game is over.

# Looking Good, Feeling Fine

Looking good and feeling fine go hand in hand. When you're healthy, it shows, and you have all the extra energy you need to be a good cheerleader. To feel your best, you must take care of yourself. This means establishing good eating habits, getting plenty of exercise, and determining the amount of sleep that's right for you. Eat three balanced meals a day, and drink six to eight glasses of water to replenish moisture lost through perspiration.

Nutrition experts agree that your body is like a car that runs on fuel. Each of its cells must be nourished to keep it going strong. At least forty-five nutrients are needed for efficient body functioning, but no single food offers all the essentials. Your hair, skin, teeth, nails, and the rest of your body need certain nutrients to work and look their best. Therefore, make sure your daily diet includes a fresh egg, two servings of cereal or whole-grain bread, butter or margarine, and four servings of fresh fruit and high-vitamin vegetables. Then, since a neat appearance is a must for a cheerleader, all you have to do is make the most of how you look.

Start with a professional haircut that suits your height, face shape, hair type, and you. Try a versatile length that you won't get bored with (for girls one that you can pull off your face or anchor with barrettes). A cut that conforms to your hair's natural bend will swing into place with little fuss.

Hair should be in top condition. Dry, droopy hair that's plagued with split ends is nothing to cheer about. Once cheerleading starts making its rigorous demands on your hair, you

221

must shampoo frequently to remove perspiration buildup and grime. Shampoo as often as necessary to keep your hair from looking straggly or clumping together. Look for a shampoo that's especially formulated for your hair type, which will make it look its very best.

Every time you wash your hair you should condition it also. Conditioning is vital to hair that's getting more than its share of washing, brushing, blow-drying, or curling. In fact, it's a good idea to have a deep-conditioning treatment whenever your hair is professionally trimmed. Have it trimmed regularly to keep it looking healthy and to prevent split ends from traveling up the hair shaft. For the shiniest hair, try rinsing your hair with cool water after shampooing, because hot water robs it of lubricants. Also, clean your combs and brushes as regularly as your hair.

When you're spending a lot of time outdoors in winter, your hair needs special treatment to counteract the drying effects of the weather. Too much cold can strip hair of its natural moisture and destroy its body and shine, just like too much sun. If your hair becomes super dry, shampoo only when necessary. A protein-rich shampoo will strengthen the hair, and help put it back in perfect condition.

*An aside to the girls:* Hair that doesn't move doesn't belong on the field or court. Nor does hair that's not a natural-looking color. Nothing looks worse than a blond head of hair growing from a set of black roots.

Rosy cheeks may be the healthy results of cheering outdoors in the winter, but they are also signs of parched skin. A cheerleader's skin needs special care in the winter to protect it from the damaging effects of wind and harsh weather.

If your skin feels rough, chapped, and itchy, soothe it by turning an ordinary bath into a skin treatment. Pour a capful or two of baby oil or bath oil into warm water. Meanwhile, you might put on some sort of face cream before you get into the tub. Then close your eyes and relax. Bath water should be warm, not hot. Hot water can soak the moisture out of your skin, leaving it even drier and itchier. When you get out of the tub, dry yourself off with a soft towel. Then spread body lotion over the driest parts of your body, including your toes, soles, and heels. Make a point of guarding against windburn and chapping by moisturizing your skin whenever you go out to cheer. *A word of caution:* Never bathe immediately before going outdoors or shortly after returning. Sudden temperature changes can upset the moisture balance in your skin.

Protect your skin in the summer too by wearing a sunscreen to practice when the rays of the sun are strong. The sun increases oil gland production, which may cause skin problems. To fight excess dirt before it results in pimples and blackheads, keep your face as clean as possible. And remember to reapply a moisturizer after washing.

Girls, you should wear a minimal amount of makeup for a fresh, natural appearance. Don't look like a paint box. For a healthy glow, try a touch of blush-on with just a hint of color. You can wear it over moisturizer or bare skin. Apply blusher along your cheekbone, all the way up to the hair line. Don't just smudge it on in a circle. If you want, use it for contouring your face, by keeping in mind that darker shades will make an area recede.

If you have some blemishes, don't hide them by covering your entire face with foundation. It will cake and look terrible, which is far worse than the problem you are trying to conceal. Instead, use just a dab of cover-up cream on the spots that need it and blend *well*.

Cheerleaders who look their best save most of their eye makeup for Saturday night. For games and rallies, use it sparingly. (Excessive eye makeup runs when you perspire.)

Anyone working outdoors should always use lip gloss, whether wearing lip color or not. Gloss helps protect the lips from chapping. And speaking of chapping; never lick your lips when cheering. Instead, reapply gloss (or lipstick with a built-in moisturizer) whenever there's a break in the action— in the privacy of the rest room. Don't fuss with your hair or makeup in front of the fans on the field; that's in poor taste.

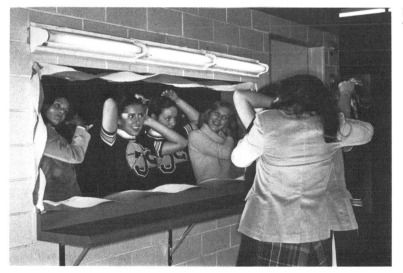

Never fuss with your hair in front of the fans.

How to face-up.

Looking poised.

Contacts aren't for everyone who needs corrective lenses, so glasses are frequently as much a part of how you look as your hair and dress. If you wear glasses, it's important to give some thought to the shape, style, and size of your frames to be sure they're flattering. But remember that they have to fit well and be able to stand up to exercise, so choose wisely.

As for your teeth, eat properly, then spend a few minutes after every meal brushing and flossing. When you can't, at least rinse your mouth with water. But, regardless of how carefully you brush, you should have your teeth cleaned professionally every six months to keep any plaque from accumulating, and to keep minor problems from becoming major ones.

The hands of a cheerleader get lots of attention, so be sure yours are well-groomed. Girls, keep nails at a reasonable length. Otherwise, they are practically guaranteed to break or hurt someone when you're cheering. Guys, yours will look best if they are short and clean.

There's a right and a wrong way to file nails. Use the fine side of an emery board to shape your nails, always filing from the sides to the center. Sawing back and forth usually causes nails to shred. Nails will be strongest if you never file down into the sides where the nail meets the skin, and if you shape them somewhat square.

When giving yourself a manicure, soak your nails in a small bowlful of warm, soapy water, or warm olive oil, for five to ten minutes to soften the cuticle. Then dry your hands and gently push back the cuticles with an orange stick. Rinse again and dry. For a finishing touch, rub your hands with some cream or lotion to make them soft.

If you don't want to polish your nails, buff them. The shine will last a week and some experts claim this is the natural way to healthier nails. If you use polish, it should be clear or blend with the color of your uniform. Chipped polish is unsightly. Nothing looks worse than seeing someone biting his or her nails. To guard against that, between cheers, stand with your hands clasped behind your back. *Another tip:* When you wash your hands in the lavatory at half time, have a moisturizer handy and put it on before going outside. Otherwise, if your hands are damp, they'll chap.

Keep your shoes clean, polished, and in good repair. This

means your heels shouldn't be worn down, or the backs saggy. If you really want to look great from head to toe, give yourself a monthly pedicure. (After all, what's good for the hands is good for the feet, especially feet that have been stuffed into cheering shoes on cold, wet nights.)

Begin by clipping toenails straight across. Next, soak your feet in a warm, soapy footbath. While your feet are damp, rub away dead, rough skin on heels and soles with a pumice stone. Rinse and push cuticles back with an orange stick. Rinse again and dry carefully before generously applying a moisturizer.

Girls, when you're cheerleading, you're almost always in motion, so people get more than a glimpse of your legs. Keep them free of hair. The best time to shave is after a bath or shower, since that's when you can get the closest shave. Also, keep your underarms fresh and smooth. (Underarm hair is a breeding ground for bacteria.)

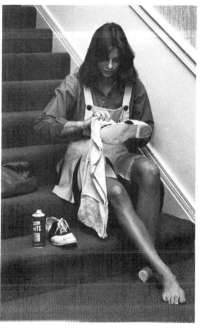

Taking a step in the right direction.

To avoid the embarrassment of both perspiration odor and wetness, everyone needs an antiperspirant. Deodorants stop odors but antiperspirants react with sweat glands to help eliminate the flow of moisture to the skin's surface.

To evaluate your posture, stand against a wall with heels, hips, and head touching it. Stretch tall. The space between your lower back and the wall should be just enough to feel the pressure of your fingertips if you tried to slide your hand through. Your posture reflects your opinion of yourself, the experts say.

When you walk, walk tall. Point your feet directly ahead and come down on your heel, then roll to your toes. You should lead with your thighs while your knees remain slightly flexed. Shoulders ought to be relaxed, palms facing your thighs. Hold your head up, let your arms swing freely, and keep your feet parallel.

If you have a tendency to walk pigeon-toed or duck-footed, find a long, straight line along the sidewalk or in any room. Then practice walking the line.

When running, keep your body straight but tilted slightly forward. Hold your shoulders naturally and your head up. Don't run on the tips of your toes—your heel should touch the ground first. Lift your legs from the thighs to develop a better stride.

## Uniforms

From the first game all the way to the play-offs, everyone needs a uniform that is comfortable.

If you've been cheering for a while, you know choosing uniforms means making a lot of important decisions—about color, style, fabric, and price. On the other hand, if you're a first-year cheerleader, you'll find it's smart to do some investigating before the squad gets together to decide on anything.

It's hard to decide if you're not sure what you want. (You name it, chances are the NCA has got it, in its Cheerleader Supply Company.*) Ask yourselves what fabric and uniform will best suit your climate, and decide on a sweater with short sleeves, long sleeves, or no sleeves—or perhaps a letter jacket. Then find out how much money you have to spend, and how many uniforms you need. Consider the shapes and sizes of those on your squad and agree on a style that flatters everyone. (The Cheerleader Supply Company has over three hundred designs to choose from—in every color.)

One of the most exciting things about being a cheerleader is getting together as a squad and choosing your uniforms.

Most squads have a game uniform for each sports season and another outfit that is worn to school on pep rally days. But all of these are not necessary, so resist the temptation to exceed your budget. And never purchase uniforms without your advisor's approval.

* To write for a catalog: Cheerleader Supply Co., P.O. Box 30175, Dallas, Texas 75262.

Girls should ask the advisor for advice when it's time to shorten their skirts. You should agree on a length that will compliment everyone. In any case, skirts should be hemmed evenly, not in a lopsided fashion. And speaking of length, be sure your shirts are long enough to stay tucked into your tights. Your tights and underwear should match your outfit, too. Don't wear red tights with a yellow skirt. Make sure your tights fit properly, so you're not always having to pull them down to keep your underwear from showing.

Don't wear a uniform that's too tight. You won't look as attractive if you're constantly tugging to keep your clothes from riding up. Furthermore, the stitching is more apt to rip.

A uniform should always be cleaned and pressed immediately after a game so it is ready to go to the next one. Also, the seams should be checked regularly.

*One last word:* As a good cheerleader, take pride in your appearance before the game, so you can concentrate on cheering during the event.

## Accessories

They've got it all together.

After settling on uniforms, turn your attention to accessories. Keep the style of your uniforms in mind when selecting shoes. Tennis shoes and track shoes are fine for practice, but when your squad is wearing its dress uniform, your whole appearance can fall flat by choosing the wrong shoe. Try the traditional saddle oxford, a Charlie Brown saddle with crepe soles, a super stripe saddle, or a megaphone wedge. They may not be good for jogging or parties, but they are good for cheerleading.

Squad members should wear the same style shoes and the same style socks, color coordinated to match their uniforms. In wet weather wear two pairs of socks to keep your feet warm. When your feet are cold, you will feel cold all over. Therefore, put on a pair of cotton anklets, then put your uniform socks over them.

Pompons (the fullest and fluffiest available), megaphones, and tote bags should be in your school colors as well. And don't wear any jewelry on the field or court, since it can be easily lost or broken and it can even be dangerous.

To be prepared to repair a hanging button or drooping hemline, always carry a needle, thread, and safety pins. Hair clips and money are also important in case of emergencies.

# Raising Necessary Funds

Few schools provide sufficient money to cover the expenses of cheerleading. As a result it's often necessary for a squad to raise money for costs such as cheerleading camp, uniforms, travel expenses, and supplies for poster making.

When planning a fund raiser, keep your purpose in mind. Know how much money you need to earn, what type project will help you reach your goal, and when and where you want this event to be held. Before you go ahead with anything, make sure you have the administration's approval. Then appoint a chairman who is responsible and reliable, who knows that organization is the key to effective fund raising, and who will readily order materials and begin publicizing the event.

## Fantastic Fund-Raising Ideas, Courtesy of the NCA

*A disco! During lunch hours in the school cafeteria have a record player, two large speakers, and plenty of records. Advertise requests and dedications for only fifteen cents per record. Publicize this activity in advance for maximum participation.*

Have a raffle for the game ball at your rally, and announce the winner at half time!

*Birthday-grams. Set up a booth in school where students give you the name, place, and date of anyone they would like to have "Happy Birthday" sung to. The same may be done for Valentine's Day, with candy-grams.*

Have a basketball game between the faculty and your squad and charge admission.

*Have a bake sale at school! Sell brownies, cupcakes, and cookies during breaks and lunch.*

Sell sweat shirts in your school colors with school name or mascot on them. When fans sit together at the game, they'll look really sharp! Also consider selling bumper stickers, miniature footballs, stuffed animals, book covers, or pens with your school's name.

*Sell parents stadium cushions with your mascot printed on them.*

Have a photographer take pictures at games, pep rallies, lunch hours, and in the halls before school during the school year. At the end of the year have a "Walk Down Memory Lane Sale" and sell all of the pictures!

*Have a Colors Day. Students not wearing school colors have to pay a fine.*

Have a "Cutest Baby Contest." Get pictures of the athletes for each sport (both girl and guy athletes). Ask that they bring a picture of themselves one year old or younger. Number them, then put them on display with their number on a jar. Students vote by putting money in the jar of the contestant of their choice (one cent equals one vote). At the end of the week have a pep rally, have the contestants dress up in baby clothes, and introduce them to the student body. Crown the Baby King and Queen of the school and parade them around the gym in little red wagons.

*Rake leaves in the fall for a fee.*

Sponsor a "Howdy Dance" to welcome the new sophomores into the swing. Hiring a disc jockey is much less expensive than having a band.

*Sell spirit blocks. Cut colored construction paper into pieces the size of the tiles on the hall walls. Sell them for ten cents each, then have students write messages on them and stick them on the walls for spirited halls.*

Sell "Pride Pins" to parents of the players. A button about three and a half inches in diameter has room for writing "My son is number 8," "My daughter is great," or something similar.

*Have a nearby restaurant put out coupon books with your mascot name on the front of them, then sell them for a profit, thus also giving the restaurant business.*

Have a dog wash.

*Hold a cheerleading clinic for elementary students in*

*neighboring communities and another one for those in junior high.*

If your school films any of your sporting events, talk with your coaches and see if they would permit your squad to show a game film to the student body. The best games would be any that were out of town, which many students would not have been able to attend. You could charge an admission fee and show it in the high school auditorium.

# Administering First Aid

As an athlete, you know the importance of total body fitness. Also, research indicates that lack of physical fitness is a major cause of sports injury. But, even when an individual is in great shape, unexpected injuries and illnesses can occur. To minimize your chances of being hurt, don't try to be a hero when you aren't feeling well. If another cheerleader is not feeling up to par, be prepared with some medical know-how. Good sense and quick action will help you act confidently and efficiently when emergencies arise. The NCA offers these first-aid basics.

## Fracture

If there's a bone protruding through the skin, an inability to move a movable part of the body, or pain following the twist of a joint, the injury may be a fracture. DO NOT MOVE the injured, unless it is necessary to protect him or her from further injury. Instead, keep the victim still, and seek a physician at once.

## Sprained Ankle (or Any Muscle Injury)

If you think someone has sprained an ankle or any other muscle, have him or her elevate the ankle, and apply a cold pack or ice wrapped in a towel. (Cold inhibits swelling by narrowing the arteries and restricting blood flow. If there's little blood seeping into the tissues, there's little swelling.) Continue for approximately one hour, then put on an elastic

233

wrap. If pain persists, it's best that the victim asks his or her own doctor for advice. If the strain is slight, and the swelling is gone by the end of the day, avoid putting excessive weight on sprain. Apply heat after twenty-four hours.

## Nosebleed

Although a nosebleed generally looks far worse than it is, do keep the victim calm. Most ear, nose, and throat specialists recommend the bleeder place cotton in the nostrils and apply pressure to the nose. Head should be tilted forward, *not* backward, so blood doesn't go into the throat. You can help by rinsing the victim's face off with warm water as soon as possible.

## Other Bleeding

Cleanse the wound with all-purpose antiseptic. Place Band-Aid or gauze over the wound and apply direct pressure for at least five minutes. Then change the dressing. If the wound requires stitches, seek medical help.

## Insect Bites

If the stinger is visible, remove it with sterilized tweezers or by scraping the point of a sterilized needle over the skin. Use a cotton swab and all-purpose antiseptic to clean the bite. Then apply a cold compress to relieve discomfort. WARNING: Some people are allergic to insect bites. If excessive swelling, dizziness, or breathing difficulty occurs, get prompt medical assistance.

## Heat Exhaustion

Hot and humid weather can have adverse effects on the body, and so can cheering in a poorly ventilated gymnasium. Therefore, when the temperature is near ninety degrees, and the humidity is hovering around the 75-percent mark, it makes good sense to take it easy. Tiredness, dizziness, headache, and nausea, together with (or without) profuse perspiration, are all warning signs of heat exhaustion. If an individual ignores the warning symptoms, the condition rapidly worsens. To help relieve discomfort, offer a salt solution (one-half teaspoon salt per one-half glass water) every fifteen minutes for one hour while victim rests, preferably flat on his or her back with legs elevated to improve blood circulation to the brain and the rest of the body. The victim may also be cooled by towels to help lower body temperature. If symptoms persist, consult a doctor.

## Heat Cramps

Heat cramps often accompany heat exhaustion. Apply direct pressure on the abdominal muscles or limbs with warm, wet towels. Offer the victim a salt solution. And if cramps persist, seek medical care.

## Hyperventilation

Hyperventilation sometimes occurs when a person is over-excited. An excessive rate and depth of respiration leads to abnormal loss of carbon dioxide from the blood and causes the hyperventilator to feel as though he or she cannot get enough air. In truth, the individual is getting too much. Urge the victim to relax. Then "cup" your hands over the person's nose and mouth so that he or she begins breathing carbon dioxide. Patient should readily respond with normal breathing. WARNING: If victim resumes vigorous activity too soon, hyperventilating may occur again.

## Fainting

Overdoing it can cause fainting—a reaction of the nervous system that temporarily reduces the blood supply to the brain. If someone feels faint, have him or her lie flat. If space prohibits victim from doing so, have him or her lower his or her head between the knees and breathe deeply. If the person has fainted, keep the victim lying flat for ten or more minutes even though consciousness normally returns immediately. Should it not, seek medical attention at once. In the event that fainting occurs frequently, individual should consult a physician.

Get in the habit of carrying a first-aid kit to all games and practices. (Or have the head cheerleader be responsible for doing so.) Ask your doctor or pharmacist about what necessities to stock. Mentioned here is a list of items that are handy to have: aspirin, Band-Aids, elastic wrap, all-purpose antiseptic, cotton, adhesive tape, thermometer, salt tablets, sunscreen, sanitary needs, scissors, tweezers, sterile gauze pads, sterilized needle, contact lens solution, and Kleenex.

# Displaying Leadership and Responsibility

Your leadership ability is tested at sporting events. It doesn't take long for you to know if you make the grade. The crowd will look to you if you have proven knowledgeable about the game, but it will ignore you if you do not know what is happening on the field or you don't respond intelligently.

Don't forget, it's your responsibility to understand the rules and signals of every sport for which you cheer, and to draw from your list of cheers wisely.

The NCA recommends that you select a captain from the squad after you have worked together as cheerleaders for a few weeks. The captain assumes responsibility for the squad and works with the advisor. The preferred way would be for cheerleaders to vote for the natural leader who has emerged. The NCA frowns upon automatically naming the spiritleader with the most school votes as head cheerleader.

The NCA lists these duties of the head cheerleader:

- Set a good example for the squad, then be certain all cheerleaders obey the rules and regulations of cheerleading.

- Relay all messages from the advisor.

- Clear all decisions with the advisor.

- Call for a vote when there's a disagreement within the squad. Even then the advisor has the final say.

- Be responsible for the pep rally program. Welcome suggestions.

237

- Clear arrangements for after-game parties and money-making projects with the advisor and/or administrator.

- Be sure the advisor is informed of a cheerleader's illness during a game.

- With the advisor, handle all arrangements for tryouts—including tryout information, clinics, judges.

- Check that squad members maintain their academic averages.

- With the sponsor's help, order uniforms.

- Keep a notebook of activities.

- Call special meetings.

- Be sure squadmates know the signals for each sport used by the referees.

- Select appropriate cheers and chants during the game.

- Obtain and return flags for home game flag ceremonies.

- Make sure there are refreshments for the visiting cheerleaders.

- Be certain the squad leaves the floor or field when the official gives the signal, even though a cheer may be incomplete.

- Recognize potential unsportsmanlike situations and do whatever is necessary to smooth them over.

- Choose formations wisely.

- Make sure the dressing rooms are picked up after the game.

- At the game, politely request that no one take pictures of a player shooting a foul shot. Otherwise a player's vision may be blurred by the flash.

- Be sure cheerleaders cheer positively, not negatively, never putting down an opponent.

Cheerleaders should be responsible for their own conduct at all times. They should also keep their parents informed of activities relating to the group. Cheerleaders should encourage other students to try out for the squad and be sure unsuccessful candidates are invited to join the pep club and assist in poster making.

Welcoming the visiting team and their cheerleaders as guests of your school is an important responsibility. A cheerleader's attitude and actions toward a rival school has a strong influence on the attitude and actions of the rest of the student body. Besides, you'll want to use this opportunity to help promote a good relationship between schools. Here are some points for being a good host:

- Arrive at least one hour before a home game so you are ready to welcome your rivals at the door when they arrive.

- Greet them with a smile.

- Show them where they are to cheer and where the restrooms are located.

- Talk about alternating cheers if you share a common side. Maybe suggest they cheer first during time-outs in the first and third quarters and you do the same during the second and fourth periods.

- Treat your guests with the same respect and consideration you would choose to have them treat you.

- Have a special hello yell be your first cheer.

- Encourage students from your school to welcome the opposing cheerleaders with applause when exchanging yells.

Top cheerleaders aren't content to simply let things happen. That's not their style. They *make* things happen. There is a knack to achieving success, and the best cheerleaders know that the more they put into cheerleading, the more they—and everyone else—will get out of it.

# Appendix: Sample Constitution

I. PURPOSE

Cheerleaders shall promote school spirit and develop good sportsmanship among the student body and better relations between schools in the conference.

II. THE SQUADS
1. There shall be one varsity squad composed of eight students who are juniors and seniors.
2. There shall be one junior varsity squad composed of eight freshman and sophomores, unless a freshman squad is elected to cheer for all freshman teams. Then junior varsity squad will be made up of sophomores only.
3. Each squad will have a head cheerleader selected by squadmates and approved by advisor, and also a co-head cheerleader. Both will be responsible for leading and guiding the squad in accordance with its purpose.

III. UNIFORMS
1. Cheerleaders are responsible for uniform costs that exceed money allotted by the School Board.
2. Prior to being ordered, uniforms must be approved by the advisor.
3. Uniforms are to be cleaned after each game, as are cheering shoes.
4. Uniforms are to be worn only for games and rallies, unless permission is granted by the advisor.

IV. GAMES

1. Cheerleaders must attend ALL home and away football and basketball games.
2. Cheerleaders must arrive at least thirty minutes before each game.

V. TRANSPORTATION

1. Cheerleaders must travel to and from away games in transportation provided by the school.
2. Permission to travel with parents must be accompanied by a note from parent and approved by advisor.

VI. PRACTICES

1. Attendance at practice is required.
2. It is each cheerleader's responsibility to be "stretched" by the time practice begins.

VII. CONDUCT

1. Cheerleaders should conduct themselves as official student representatives of the school.
2. They should not smoke, drink alcoholic beverages, or use profanity while in uniform.
3. They should act in sportsmanlike manner at all times and discourage any unsportsmanlike conduct of boosters.
4. Cheerleaders should willingly cooperate with head cheerleader, squadmates, advisor, coaches, and the administration.

VIII. REQUIREMENTS

1. To remain eligible to cheer, cheerleaders must maintain at least a "C" average in each subject and satisfactory citizenship grades.
2. All cheerleaders must attend summer camp with the squad.
3. All cheerleaders are required to have a physical examination prior to camp.

IX. DISMISSAL

1. A cheerleader shall be dismissed for smoking or drinking alcoholic beverages in uniform.
2. A cheerleader may be dismissed for unbecoming conduct that reflects poorly on the school.
3. If scholastic average falls below a "C" for two grading periods, dismissal from squad will result.
4. A cheerleader will also be dismissed if he or she

accumulates twenty-five demerits. (See "Demerit System Example" following this constitution.)

X. TRYOUT PROCEDURE
1. A two-week training program will be conducted by current cheerleaders one month prior to tryouts.
2. A screening committee—made up of retiring head cheerleader, two cheerleader instructors from recognized cheerleader association, two cheerleaders from a nearby college, or two cheerleader advisors from other schools—will observe and judge the performance of all candidates and submit to the student body a list of most qualified candidates.
3. All candidates will wear numbers to designate who they are when they try out. Required will be two cheers, three different jumps, two double stunts.
4. The student body will vote for cheerleading representatives within two days of screening committee voting. Students will be given a list of candidates by name and number as they enter the gymnasium. Students will circle the names and numbers of the candidates they feel are best qualified to represent them. Ballots will be collected at the completion of the tryouts as students exit the gymnasium. Ballots will be tallied by three persons: one vice-principal, the cheerleader advisor, and one teacher.

## Demerit System Example

When a cheerleader has accumulated twenty-five demerits, he or she will be expelled from the squad. A total of ten demerits will justify suspension for one week. In this case the cheerleader will still be required to practice with the group.

"F" on report card . . . . . . . . . . . . . . . . . . . . . . . .25 Demerits
Less than "C" average . . . . . . . . . . . . . . . . . . . . . .25
Attending out-of-town game without parental
  permission . . . . . . . . . . . . . . . . . . . . . . . . . . . . .25
Not attending scheduled game . . . . . . . . . . . . . . 9
Tardy to activity . . . . . . . . . . . . . . . . . . . . . . . . . . 5
Missing practice . . . . . . . . . . . . . . . . . . . . . . . . . 5
Forgetting equipment . . . . . . . . . . . . . . . . . . . . . 4
Leaving practice early . . . . . . . . . . . . . . . . . . . . . 4
Failure to execute cheerleading assignment . . . 5

# Index